FROM BATTLE SCARS TO
Beauty Marks

To inquire about Ellie's speaking or
writing ministry,
please contact
HEART MIND & SOUL MINISTRIES
Ellie Lofaro
PO Box 9292
Reston, VA 20195
Phone/Fax 703.435.5334
Web: www.ellielofaro.com
Booking: info@ellielofaro.com
Questions: assistant@ellielofaro.com

Other books by Ellie Lofaro

Leap of Faith

This book is filled with biblical truth, poignant personal stories, bottom-line honesty, and profound take-home value. With her characteristic humor woven through every chapter, Ellie Lofaro teaches us how to survive in a fallen world. Whether on the platform as a speaker or as a writer of substance, Ellie is one of the finest communicators of our time.

—*Carol Kent, author and president of Speak Up!*

Bonding with the Blonde Women

Like a beautiful tapestry, Ellie Lofaro's book weaves together true (sometimes hilarious) stories from life that manifest the threads of God's grace—threads that hold us together even when life seems to be falling apart. Wrap this book around your heart and discover again what it means to be under the blanket of God's love.

—*Janet Parshall, host of "Janet Parshall's America"*

Slices of Life

Sitting down with this book is like chatting on the phone with a friend who trusts you enough to tell you what she really thinks. And what does Ellie Lofaro think? From resolutions to bumper stickers, bonbons to lice, God is precisely where we are so sure He cannot be. He is in our midst—in the ordinary events of our lives. I love this book!

—*Barbara Johnson, best-selling author and speaker*

FROM BATTLE SCARS TO
Beauty Marks

Portraits of Women Who
Turned Trials to Triumphs

ELLIE LOFARO

LIFE JOURNEY®

Bringing Home the Message for Life

COOK COMMUNICATIONS MINISTRIES
Colorado Springs, Colorado • Paris, Ontario
KINGSWAY COMMUNICATIONS LTD
Eastbourne, England

Life Journey® is an imprint of
Cook Communications Ministries, Colorado Springs, CO 80918
Cook Communications, Paris, Ontario
Kingsway Communications, Eastbourne, England

From Battle Scars to Beauty Marks
© 2006 by Ellie Lofaro

First printing, 2006
Printed in the United States of America

3 4 5 6 7 8 9 10 11 Printing/Year 10 09 08 07 06

Unless otherwise noted, Scripture quotations are taken from the HOLY
BIBLE, NEW INTERNATIONAL VERSION®. Copyright © 1973, 1978,
1984 International Bible Society. Used by permission of Zondervan. All
rights reserved. Scripture quotations marked "NKJV™" are taken from the
New King James Version®. Copyright © 1982 by Thomas Nelson, Inc.
Used by permission. All rights reserved; (NASB) taken from the New
American Standard Bible®, Copyright © 1960, 1995 by The Lockman
Foundation. Used by permission. (www.Lockman.org); (KJV) are from the
King James Version of the Bible. (Public Domain); (CEV) are taken from
the Contemporary English Version Copyright © 1995 by American Bible
Society. Used by permission.

Library of Congress Cataloging-in-Publication Data

Lofaro, Ellie.
   From battle scars to beauty marks : portraits of women who turned tri-
als to triumphs / Ellie Lofaro.-- 1st ed.
     p. cm.
   ISBN-13: 978-0-7814-4169-8
   ISBN-10: 0-7814-4169-2
   1. Christian women--United States--Biography. 2. Christian women--
Religious life. I. Title.
BR1713.L64 2006
248.8'6'0922--dc22

                                        2005021823

For Patsy Clairmont

*Thank you for granting access to your battle scars as
well as your beauty marks.
It's obvious you have embraced and been
enlightened by each one.
Your transparency has brought hope and
healing to millions of women
… including me.*

*Be it a battle or a parade—
I'll be marching right behind you.*

With love and deep admiration …

Contents

Acknowledgments

Besides the usual and (deeply deserved) debt of gratitude I owe to my dear husband and children, I would like to offer my heartfelt appreciation to the very fine people of

Cook Communications Ministries
and
Cook Communications Ministries International.

Your passion to see the gospel go forth to the ends of the earth has steadily comforted, convicted, and centered my own personal reasons for writing books.

Though there are "miles to go before we sleep," it is fitting to rest from time to time and celebrate God's goodness and continual provision.

May the vision increase and the mission be blessed.

Thank you for allowing me to travel with you these past five years.

I have grown along the way.

Foreword

What an incredible journey it is to live on this planet called earth with a deep ache for our real home called heaven. No matter how much we may experience joy, there is always the realization of sorrow and heartache because we are not in "the garden." We were made for another world and this isn't it. There are tears and sickness. There is war and evil. There is always the uncertainty of a new day that will hold its own trouble. In the midst of great uncertainty, our greatest certainty is Jesus. A constant companion, a giver of courage, a true friend and healer.

Thus comes the paradox of Christian living. Die to live. Love when you don't feel like it because it will produce more love. Forgive when you have been hurt because you will loosen your own chains. We trust in a God who says He is trustworthy even when the future looks bleak because He is the only One who holds the future.

So we continue in this battleground knowing that—in the midst of wounds and brokenness, storms and sleeplessness, fear and sorrow—He will work it *all* out for good. Somehow the Lord uses pain as His pen to write our stories for our ultimate good and for His glory. He *is* trustworthy and even when we don't hold on, He doesn't let go.

I love the account of Peter walking on water. The minute he lost faith he began to sink. The Scriptures indicate that Jesus loved him, reached for him, and brought him back in the boat for He did not want Peter to lose hope, or faith, or his very life. Jesus didn't shame him, chastise him, or leave him. He reached for him.

I have sunk in my own moments of despair. I have weathered many storms and have known deep sorrow. I have felt helpless and in the dark. The beauty of the gospel is that when we are at our end, the Lord is just beginning. Water turns into wine, blind men see, and stones roll away. He brings a word, a letter, a person, a song, a new day. He finds a way to snatch us from our pit to put us back on the path of His promises. We need only to keep our hands open so He could slip His in and lead us on to higher ground.

There is nothing more powerful in communicating God's miraculous grace and strength than through real lives and real situations. Beauty for ashes? Is it a fairy tale someone wrote to tickle our dream driven hearts? No—it is a promise made by God. And it is true. He keeps every promise. He does not disappoint.

Ellie Lofaro has masterfully conveyed these truths through the terrible and wonderful real life stories of seven women. You will experience gut-wrenching emotions as well as hopeful relief as she meticulously conveys each woman's journey. And, in her characteristic style, you will feel as though you are walking beside them through it all. You are about to enter into very private reflections of seven brave women. Ellie manages to capture the details of their expressions with vivid, candid, sometimes unsettling imagery. You will see and feel and hear. And just when you are saying softly, "That's me," Ellie will give you an opportunity to come to terms with your own battle scars in chapter eight. She even offers a tried-and-true, fool-proof prescription for lasting beauty.

Sit back and soak in Ellie's newest gift to us. It is a labor of love, and I know you will be truly blessed, as I was. Want to turn your trials into triumphs? Read on and let your soul be encouraged. You, as well as those you love, can walk in grace, peace, and loveliness as you allow God to turn your Battle Scars into Beauty Marks.

KATHY TROCCOLI
SPEAKER, AUTHOR, RECORDING ARTIST

Habakkuk's Cry

How long, O LORD, must I call for help, but you do not listen? Or cry out to you, "Violence!" but you do not save? Why do you make me look at injustice? Why do you tolerate wrong? Destruction and violence are before me; there is strife, and conflict abounds.

—HABAKKUK 1:2–3

God's Reply

Look … and watch—and be utterly amazed. For I am going to do something in your days that you would not believe, even if you were told.

—HABAKKUK 1:5

From Battle Scars to Beauty Marks

Many fine authors and teachers have addressed one particularly complex and often painful question. It's not a question that would be—or should be—easily answered. It's not a question that produces a logical fill-in-the-blank response. But it is a question that most of us ask many times along life's path. The question is *why?*

Why the pain, suffering, and sorrow? Why earthquakes, disease, and death? Why starvation, famine, and floods? Why war, terrorism, and tyranny? (And those just covers the evening news!) On a more personal level, people struggle with bankruptcy, divorce, unresolved emotions, depression, family strife, work-related stress, poor health, fractured relationships, disintegrated self-worth, and countless other nightmares. It appears our world can be a place overwhelmed with darkness as deep as midnight.

We may be comfortable blaming pollution on greed, cirrhosis of the liver on excessive drinking, and genocide on evil despots—but what do we say of the family that drowns in a flash flood or of a baby born with severe deformity? How do we deal with the child who enthusiastically waits for the school bus only to be killed by a falling tree? How can we come to terms when a woman who survived a double mastectomy is felled by a sniper's bullet? What do we say to the mother who was victimized by a home invasion and raped alongside her teenage daughter? How do we come to terms with the loss of a quarter of a million lives in a tsumani?

We've all heard stark as well as sensitive responses to the problem of pain from people of faith. I've been told, "Man has sinned, and so we live in a fallen world that is hurtling toward death and destruction." I've also heard this response: "We can never know all the mysteries of life, but God is close when we suffer and has made a way for us to live with Him forever in paradise."

As one who believes the Holy Bible to be true and reliable, I accept both these statements, though the first doesn't go over well in "mixed company" of believers and nonbelievers. The problem for me—and for most people I meet in my travels—is that neither answer brings great comfort to those enduring a season of suffering.

This problem of pain has kept philosophers and theologians busy for thousands of years, and I don't expect that to change anytime soon. The question *Why?* will continue to challenge thinking men and women whether they believe that God is their reason for living or that God doesn't exist. Let's just agree that pain and suffering are difficult and consistent realities in the journey called life. The truth is that the human condition is both fragile and resilient, feeble and mighty, filled with hope as well as despair.

In this book I will not attempt to answer the *why* you are grappling with. I'm grappling too. But I've come to understand that our lives are a series of stories. In addition to stories of joy, victory, celebration, and love, many of our stories are painful ones. Some are unspeakable. All have a profound effect on who we are, what we think, and how we face the future. As a Christian, I can confidently attest to the fact that faith does not inoculate one from trouble. As a middle-aged woman, I have lived long enough to observe that no one escapes pain and suffering.

So, if trusting God (and His Son Jesus) doesn't spare us from difficulty and death during our time on the planet, is there any comfort to be found in faith? I believe there is.

What a mighty God we serve.

There's power in the blood.

Abundant life.

Peace that passes understanding.

Rejoice in the Lord.

God is so good.

Ministering angels are always with us.

I've got joy deep down in my heart.

It is well with my soul.

The name of the Lord is a strong tower.

Have you heard those expressions from Christians? Have you spoken them? I have. After almost fifty years in the classroom of life, I have personally made some less-than-scientific but highly reliable observations. People with deep faith are not exempt from trials and heartaches, but they handle emotional and physical hardships very differently than those without faith. We have all heard the medical data proving that faith causes the body to heal more fully and at an accelerated pace. Faith results in stronger marriages and better business practices. Faith provides hope and confidence and many other good gifts.

Besides being an author, I have the privilege of speaking at conferences from coast to coast. I also have the unique joy of teaching a weekly interdenominational Bible study. In the course of life, I meet many women and hear their many stories. I am often left speechless upon learning of their tragedies and left breathless as they share their triumphs. There is one thing the "victors" all have in common: an utter devotion to and trust in the goodness, grace, and greatness of God. They are completely convinced of His love for them—even though their painful stories might lead doubters to different conclusions.

It is imperative that these stories be told, and that is why I am writing this book.

Recounted in these pages are the true accounts of seven amazing "she-roes." Forget Superwoman, Wonder Woman, or Xena the Warrior Princess. These women are the real deal, the genuine article, the salt of the earth. Each woman is a true warrior who affirms that her relationship with the eternal King has rewarded her richly. Forget the extreme makeovers, the island survivors, and the bachelorette who gets a rose. The stories you are about to read are truly inspiring, and I trust they will bring you hope and courage for your own road.

It was a privilege to talk intimately with these women. Everybody's story is different. Everybody's circumstances are different. Some of the topics of conversation included struggles that are common to so many: a troubled marriage, spouse, or child. But there is uniqueness in every testimony in this book.

I asked each woman I interviewed to think about her unique experience and what she wanted others to know, learn, realize, or take away from her experience. "What," I would ask, "do you want somebody in your situation to know? What do you know now that you wish you had known then?" Their answers reflect that they do not see themselves as role models, but rather as those who have fought the battles that came their way, aided by a God who would not leave their side.

Though I am unable to provide answers for the *why* of unexpected losses, I believe I have gained some valuable insights to the question that follows afterward: *How?* How did these women rise high above their pain and sorrow? How did their grief cause them to become better instead of bitter? How did they gain the resolve to be torchbearers in order to help others who are on similar paths? How did they choose victory over victimization? How have hope and healing been born of their hardships? In short, how do these women thrive when others in similar circumstances barely survive?

In speaking intimately with these brave and generous women, I noticed a clear pattern emerging. They had all faced a painful time. For some it was a moment, for others it was a season. Some still live with difficult circumstances. Yet each woman has refused to allow her pain to control or define her life.

I once saw a sign deep in the woods that pointed the way to "Midnight Pass." At that moment I was struck by a new picture of God's love, a love that leads us through our darkest night, over the massive mountain of pain and fear to safety on the other side. The One who cares and provides for you becomes your personal Midnight Pass. Scripture, poetry, and prose all speak of valleys, darkness, places where we cannot see our next steps let alone the long and winding road ahead. But God has made a way and cleared a path for us to walk through valleys of deepest darkness.

I am so pleased to honor each woman in this book and to share her story. Some portion of their lives may be very similar to yours or echo experiences of people you love. Although the stories contained in these pages describe experiences of sorrow and pain, this is first and foremost a book of encouragement and hope.

As you enter into each woman's journey, you will see signposts along the way in the form of helpful Bible passages. Stop and ponder them, and consider how they shed God's guidance and light onto your own personal path. I trust these reminders and promises from the Word of God will relate to your life and the battles you face. My hope is that you will be as encouraged and blessed as I have been by these women of deep faith.

The interviews yielded thirty hours of recorded tapes. The recorded tapes resulted in hundreds of pages of transcription. My challenge was to reduce six hundred pages down to approximately two hundred without losing the story line. And speaking of the story line, did you know that women do not generally relate the details of their lives in any particular chronological order? Needless to say, I now have a *much* deeper appreciation for editors! My desire was to be the least intrusive as possible during the interview itself.

Please note that chapter 8 is all about *you!* It's a summary of what the brave women in this book have taught us and helpful suggestions for you to apply timeless truths to your own life. It is my prayer that you will also benefit from the Readers' Guide.

The following seven accounts are true and very personal. For obvious reasons, the names of the women (as well as those of their families and friends) have been changed to protect and respect their privacy. This was not their request, but I am sure you would agree that it is a wise decision. Actually, each of these hearty souls would be glad to share her testimony one-on-one.

Isn't that how we heal and grow? Aren't you grateful for those "mighty mamas" who have come alongside to tell you that you are going to make it through that valley—and that "everything's gonna be all right"? May you seek God's will for the time and place you are to share your *own* story of how He has brought you through your darkest hours. We must never allow our churches to become country clubs when God intended for them to be hospitals!

To some extent, we *all* carry the battle scars of life. Let's trust God to help us look past those temporal, though often deep, scars in favor of the beauty marks that are deeper still. Thanks to the Creator's tender love and care, those who choose to turn trials into triumphs receive eternal beauty marks that no person or circumstance can *ever* take away.

Seven women. Seven stories. Seven struggles. Seven broken hearts. Seven miracles. Seven deaths and seven resurrections. Seven soulful, joyful, colorful, grateful, hopeful, spiritual, wonderful, God-filled women. Listen in …

The kind of faith God values seems to develop best when everything fuzzes over, when God stays silent, when the fog rolls in.

—Philip Yancey

CHAPTER ONE

Barbara: Giving Unconditional Love

$\mathcal{B}$arbara is petite, stylish, southern, and sassy. In her mid-forties, she still has that cheerleader personality she established while growing up in the heartland of Texas, a place she proudly refers to as "the great country of Texas." She and her husband Rob and their two children now live in an affluent Houston suburb. Her daughter, Meg, is twenty and thriving in college. Her son, Jeff, is twenty-four and serving time in prison for various drug-related crimes.

Barbara's story is that of a mother's undying, unconditional, unending love for her child—even when that mother's heart is broken. Her story is also about God's unconditional love for her and her son, a love available to each of us regardless of our needs and failings.

When we talked, I asked Barbara to describe her son. She said that Jeff looks like a model from a Gap commercial. He was a white-blond towhead as a little boy, and she still sees that little boy when she thinks of him. Blessed with a wonderful sense of humor, Jeff has always loved life; he's a real survivor with a strong connection to his mother.

Though a very bright person, Jeff has battled Attention

Deficit/Hyperactivity Disorder (ADHD) and learning disabilities. He is extremely intelligent, but he learns differently, which has created problems most of his life. He had to leave a Christian elementary school because they could not facilitate his special needs. He attended a private school for children with learning disabilities.

Barbara picks up her story here.

In Her Own Words: Barbara's Story

Jeff experienced a great deal of shame in his early years. He would say, "I ride the short bus." School was a struggle. He'd say, "I am so tired of everybody telling me to sit still! I get so tired of having to be still and be quiet." Once he came home from his new school, where all the children had some sort of learning problem, and said, "Mom, we went on a field trip, and the kids today said I have a disability. Do I have a disability?"

I remember praying, "Oh God, this is one of those moments I need to know the right words to say." And God gave me the wisdom to respond, "Absolutely, Jeff, and so does Mom. Look in my eyes—I have contact lenses on. I don't see well without them. I have a disability. You don't learn the same way others learn. Now you have a choice. You can lie down and cry that you have a disability, or you can stand up and learn with the help that is given to you. We all have disabilities."

"Okay, Mom." His deep trust in me always made me want to be more trustworthy.

A Tough Childhood

Jeff was a very difficult child to raise because of his hyperactivity. He was never rude or mean-spirited, but he was always in trouble because he couldn't stay on target, or he would forget, or he never settled down. He hated birthday parties because he became so wound up and ended up being ostracized or disciplined.

When Jeff was seven, I read him and my daughter Meg *The Chronicles of Narnia*. When I finished a chapter, he would beg, "Read me more, Mom! Read me more!"

Also, I spoon-fed him the book of Proverbs. God must have looked down and smiled, because when the kids were little, there was not much quiet time for me. I would get up at five and read my verses from Proverbs and pray over the kids. Yes, both kids were hearing "Jesus lives." Jeff was very evangelistic as a little boy. He would invite the neighbors to go to church, and he would pray for friends and animals.

EVERY GOOD AND PERFECT GIFT IS FROM ABOVE, COMING DOWN FROM THE FATHER OF THE HEAVENLY LIGHTS, WHO DOES NOT CHANGE LIKE SHIFTING SHADOWS.

—JAMES 1:17

He went on medication for his ADHD, and he finally learned to read. I can still hear him sitting upstairs and being so excited: "el-ah-fent—elephant! Mom, I read *elephant*!" He had that simple wonder and joy of learning to read. The Ritalin worked, but when he came off the Ritalin, he would have a rebound. He would be more hyper than before because his body was used to false restraints. Ritalin doesn't make everything go away. We finally got permission to stay on Ritalin through evenings and weekends because he would bounce off walls and become almost unbearable.

One summer, we did a "drug holiday," when Jeff was off the medication. The only way we could survive was that I kept him in the pool where he could bounce and splash. He bounced all summer, until finally he said, "Mom, can I please go back on the medicine?" He was tired because there was no filter system for him to find rest. You and I can sit in a room and block out the buzz of the computer, the clock ticking, or the annoying fly. But when you are ADHD, you take in every stimulus. It's hard to focus, and you get so tired of your brain being on constant overdrive. He also dealt with some obsessive-compulsive behavior, and he wanted to act on everything. He was exhausted. That is why so many people with these issues eventually self-medicate. Jeff's school years were rough.

He was compliant, except for his "normal" hyperactive behavior. He got in trouble because he did something on the bus that was stupid—not fighting or drugs but mischievous stuff, being too playful. He didn't know when to stop. In the seventh and eighth grades he wanted to go to a "real" school. He fought the medication. He fought going to the small private school.

So in the seventh and eighth grades, Jeff attended a huge public middle school where there were thousands of children. In seventh grade he did well. He even got the "Most Improved" award.

In the ninth grade Jeff went out for freshman football and took down big guys because he has such heart, but he was still very little for his age. He didn't hit puberty until he was eighteen. So he was this little skinny blond kid asking, "Mom, could I get a tattoo?" He wanted to be a man. He felt a lot was working against him; he felt stupid because he was in a track for kids with learning disabilities. He was embarrassed that we had financial means and that his dad picked him up in a Mercedes for equestrian lessons. And he was small, so he was getting picked on. For protection, he started running with the "Boys in the Hood," a gang that took him in. They thought he was a novelty, this white-haired, aggressive little kid. These

African-American kids accepted him. He was the token white boy, and he made them laugh.

He picked up skateboarding skills and the clothing to match. I said, "Jeff, there is nothing wrong with a board on wheels, but there is something about this skateboard stuff I don't like." What we first noticed was he was not coming home on the school bus.

In ninth grade he began to dip. We were getting calls from the principal's office. And yet, the school officials were kind; they knew we were trying to do all the right things. I was not trying to rescue and defend my son. I was honest with them. And they knew we weren't saying, "My poor baby, he didn't do it."

The principal would ask, "What do you want? Do you want for me to suspend him? Do you want to keep him home? Do you want to keep him here? What do you think would be best this time?"

Just before drugs entered the picture, probably toward the end of Jeff's eighth-grade year, God woke me one night. I know it was God because I kept wanting to go back to sleep. God was saying, "Get up and pray for Jeff." I kept saying, "No, no, no."

Then—in my fog—it started dawning on me. "Wait a minute! This wouldn't be the Enemy waking me up to pray for Jeff. I had better get up and pray." So I dragged myself upstairs and went into his bedroom.

Jeff sat right up and said, "It's over there, Mom, in the corner! It is over there in the corner!"

I knew for sure God had sent me to be with Jeff, because in spite of Jeff's fear, I had such peace. I asked, "What's in the corner, son?"

"There's something demonic in the corner, Mom. It's over in the corner, and it's trying to get in through my eyes."

I felt God's complete peace, and I knew just what to do. We

called on the name of Jesus, and I reminded Jeff he is covered by the blood of Calvary. He said, "Right, Mom." He prayed and then I prayed over him.

I said, "Now, go on back to sleep," and I went downstairs and slept all night. In the morning when I woke up, I thought, *What happened last night? Was that real?*

I reflected on the fact that darkness enters in through the lust of the eyes, the lust of the flesh, and the pride of life—the three origins of sin. Proverbs states that it enters in through our eyes. I prayed; I did all I thought I needed to do. Prayer and more prayer.

Years later, I heard a powerful sermon on the blood of Jesus. I've always wrestled with what happened that night. I pled the blood—didn't it work? Didn't I do it right? Did I do enough? I know that kind of thinking leads to trust in our works rather than in God. I am fully confident that just as in Exodus, the blood of the Lamb is sufficient. And it was sufficient over Jeff—unless he willfully chose to open the door to that darkness.

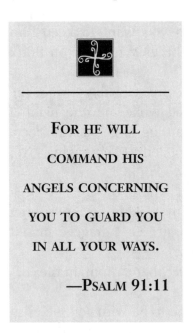

FOR HE WILL

COMMAND HIS

ANGELS CONCERNING

YOU TO GUARD YOU

IN ALL YOUR WAYS.

—PSALM 91:11

We got a call late one night when Jeff was in ninth grade. It was his soccer coach, who also happened to be a friend and neighbor. He said, "Jeff is on drugs. I just have to tell you."

I remember right where I was when I heard it. I was standing in the dining room, where I had gone to take the call for privacy. My heart sank. "Oh, Don, you're wrong! I've already asked Jeff about that." It was the classic "parents are the last to know" situation. We saw no signs of drugs. My husband was in deep denial. Nobody wants to wake up one day to hear their kid is on drugs.

I was devastated. I knew to plead the blood of Jesus over Jeff, to bind the generational curse, to fast, to read him the Word of God. I did everything I knew to be right and godly. "Oh, God! What happened? I don't deserve this!" I cried. And a thought rose up in my heart, which I knew was from God because it was not condemning. He gently said to me, "Barbara, if you got what you deserve, you would get death."

They were not easy words, but I knew they were the truth. Somehow we think if we do everything right, everything will go smoothly. The fact that I am here and breathing is God's mercy. That night I went to bed clutching my Bible.

The Gift of a Faithful Friend

At that time, a verse from Job settled in my spirit: "Though he slay me, yet will I hope in him" (13:15). I will! I did not always feel like trusting, and there were times I said, "I trust You, Lord!" simply out of obedience. I said it out loud because I thought that would have more power, but I sure didn't always feel it!

May I tell you at this point what most of the Christians in my realm were doing to me? I needed guidance, and I was getting deeper into trouble with Jeff. How do I parent? What do I do? What do I not do? My husband was dealing with being a workaholic and a gambler. I was hoping families from church would stand behind me and cheer me on, but instead, they were standing over Jeff and me loading their rifles. You know, we love to shoot our wounded! Of course, that wasn't true about everybody, but it made me distrusting and hurt.

I had a best friend, a dear, strong Christian, and even among the other friends, she was the one I knew would not

FIND REST, O MY SOUL, IN GOD ALONE; MY HOPE COMES FROM HIM. HE ALONE IS MY ROCK AND MY SALVATION; HE IS MY FORTRESS, I WILL NOT BE SHAKEN. MY SALVATION AND MY HONOR DEPEND ON GOD; HE IS MY MIGHTY ROCK, MY REFUGE. TRUST IN HIM AT ALL TIMES, O PEOPLE; POUR OUT YOUR HEARTS TO HIM, FOR GOD IS OUR REFUGE.

—PSALM 62:5–8

judge me or offer cheap advice. The only thing she would say to me was, "It will be okay." That was all I needed to hear. I did not need volumes of Scripture. I did not need a sermon or a lecture and "lift yourself up by your bootstraps" or "the sun will come out tomorrow." I just needed her to say, "It will be okay," and that would bring me peace. That friend is a true gift from God.

I remember I was getting all this advice: Give him a curfew. Be strong and parent more forcefully. Let him fail. Call his bluff. Cook his goose. Take control.

I thought, *Take control? He's jumped out of the back of a moving school bus! What am I supposed to do? That is easy for you to say!*

I went to bed one night praying, "God, what do I do?" As I laid my head down on the pillow, God reassured me: "I will capture his heart." It was such a sweet gift from God because I had instant peace, the turmoil stopped, and I went right to sleep. God was going to capture his heart. That's one of the promises I've held on to over the years. Sometimes I remind God, "You told me You are going to capture Jeff's heart, and that's what I am standing on—Your Word!" I am waiting for that.

Jeff Is Sent to Wilderness Camp

Things were out of control. Jeff wasn't going to class; he was acting out and not coming home. I was working with an addiction counselor who was seeing Jeff, and he said, "We need to get him out of here. We need to see what we can do to interrupt the behavior."

Jeff was then interviewed by a woman who assessed kids and placed them all over the country. But there was no program available that was Christian in nature. I knew unless Jeff made Jesus Christ his Lord, he would struggle his whole life. I wondered, *Don't Christians ever have problems with their kids? Why can't there be a program that can also give him the Word of God—not in a plastic, religious way, but one that would lead him to a deeper, permanent change?*

As Jeff met with this woman trying to find the right program, I sat in the waiting room. I had my Bible with me and was reading the passage in Isaiah that says, "Do not look back. Do not ponder the past. I will do a new thing. I will make a way in the wilderness and rivers in the desert." (See Isaiah 43:18–19.)

The woman came out and said, "I think we need to send him to a wilderness camp."

I thought, *Oh, God already told me that. Now I understand.* I sensed God had been giving me that verse for weeks, and I was reading it again while waiting for Jeff.

So we decided to send Jeff to the wilderness camp in Colorado. But he didn't want to go. We had an answer to his drug problem; we were going to get him off drugs. Yet the whole time I was packing this list of things, like backpacks and outdoor clothing, he was filled with resentment and fighting the whole idea.

He ran away the night before he was to leave. It was during the county fair, and Jeff ran away with this other kid who is doing time today. I battled the forces of hell all that night. We had Jeff's picture sent throughout the fairgrounds. The police were looking for him; his coach who had told us Jeff was on drugs and another friend were looking too. They finally found them two days later in a park. It was a real *Starsky and Hutch* scene, where Jeff was tackled to the ground. He kicked and screamed and spit.

Once he got to the camp, the leaders put bricks in his backpack so it would be harder to run away. But there was nowhere to run. After my husband left him there, Jeff called to say it was okay. The camp was nice. He liked the people. I remember for the first time feeling guilty, and the guilt was because I was so relieved he was gone! Too much pain. Too much worry.

Reality Hits: My Son Is an Addict

When Jeff had been out there only four days, camp officials called: "We have a problem. He's been caught in the barn out back huffing gasoline." That was the day any semblance of denial broke in me. I prayed, "Dear God, he is an addict! We positively have a problem!" I don't know whether he just wanted to be bad or rebellious or whether he really needed a fix. How many years had he been doing this? How deep into an addiction can you be at sixteen? How would he ever live a normal life? How sick are you to sniff gasoline to feel better?

When they determined he had a real problem, they sent him out in a small group with a backpack to learn how to survive, to learn self-respect, to learn to trust others. It was wonderful. And on the last day, the parents could visit. So when we flew out to see him living in a tent, we were scared to death. We didn't know if he would be mad, but he just broke down like a baby and fell into our arms.

It was the last day of the twenty-one-day wilderness experience. That night, around a bonfire, everyone shared their thoughts and feelings. A lot of parents had the same thoughts we did. I was relieved. There was peace in the air. It was very healing and very good. And then we got to go to a motel together, this little fleabag in Nowhere, Colorado, where the only restaurant in town was a saloon (but they had great burgers). That night Jeff slept between my husband and me and cried in my arms most of the night, because the leaders didn't feel he was ready to transition back. They wanted him to continue with another wilderness program.

So Jeff was put on a plane by himself there in Colorado and flown to another type of wilderness camp. In hindsight, I'm not sure it did any good. It was full of state-assigned kids with deep emotional and mental problems. It was horrendous. He was sucker-punched the first day. He lived on top of a mountain throughout the winter until February; it was just ice and snow and a tent! He would say verses he had memorized as a boy to get through the day.

When he was finished there, they still didn't feel he was ready to come home. He stayed from August to February, and it would have been his junior year of high school. Next, we hoped to find a boarding school so our son wouldn't go back to bad influences at school. But it's hard to find a boarding school to take such a high-risk kid as Jeff, and so, he had to move home. The day before school was to start, he was out all night because he couldn't sleep.

When he started back to school, it went downhill fast. He wasn't going to classes, and I was getting the calls. I thought, *Here we go again.* I had hoped it would be better. On October 13, a Friday night, it was pouring rain. After midnight I got a phone call from a police detective telling me Jeff had been arrested.

Jeff was now eighteen and had never been in jail before. He was in the adult detention center with men in the holding tank on a Friday night, which is rough. Now remember, this kid had still not gone through puberty, and he was just a scrawny, little towhead. The arresting detective said, "Ma'am, we have got to get him out of here. He doesn't belong up here."

"Wait a minute, sir. I need to think. I want to maximize the severity and the consequences of this. I don't want to just get him out of there." I didn't just want to rescue him. I knew too much. God was intervening. Part of me was excited because I knew when it got really, really tough, God could work, and there was potential.

I called our attorney. "Chuck, I don't just want to get him out of there. I want to let him sit for a couple of days. I want to let this cook."

I hardly slept a wink that night. I'd like to say I slept like a baby full of faith, but I did not. The next couple of days, Jeff kept calling: "You gotta get me out of here. You gotta get me out of here, Mom." I finally turned off the phone—not because I was so heroic; I just couldn't stand to hear his voice and hear him cry. It was too much pain. I thought, *You know what, son? You got yourself there.*

My friend assured me the county jail was a relatively

DO NOT FEAR, FOR I AM WITH YOU; DO NOT BE DISMAYED, FOR I AM YOUR GOD. I WILL STRENGTHEN YOU AND HELP YOU; I WILL UPHOLD YOU WITH MY RIGHTEOUS RIGHT HAND.

—ISAIAH 41:10

safe place. Jeff was in a holding tank in isolation until he would be moved into population—if it got that far. So I let him sit and stew. Jeff later said about my not answering his calls, "It was the first time in my life that you weren't there for me, Mom." Because I didn't run to meet his need, he had to look upward.

While Jeff was in jail, he met a guard who was a believer and who gave Jeff a tract. Jeff responded, "Oh, my mom is a believer. She's a born-again Christian. I know, I know all about it; I'll take the tracts." He stuffed them into his socks and pulled them out when he got home. He told me, "The guy said, 'If your mom is a believer, what in the world, child, are you doing here? I know you know better!'" The guard pulled Jeff aside daily and planted many good seeds in him. Those kinds of things have happened all along the way. God does not forget you just because you are in jail or you have turned your back. He is right there.

Jeff Turns Twenty-one

Jeff was eventually sentenced to fifteen days in jail, but he only served four. He came home with a new lease on life. He took the money he had saved, fixed up a house in Alabama, and sold it for a profit. He put the profits into another house a little bit on the wrong side of the tracks. It didn't take long before Jeff met some guys—the wrong people in the wrong neighborhood. I realized he lived two lives. There were times the darkness clearly drew him in.

I remember one particular Christmas when there was no joy. I said, "Jeff, there is a darkness over you. I have given you to God. It is a fearful thing to fall into the hands of Almighty God. I cannot fix you. You cannot coast on your mother's faith. You are in God's hands, and may He deal and do with you what He needs to do to get you straight." Now I don't know that a mother ever wakes up and heartily embraces the fact that her son has gone down that spiral described in Romans chapter one—all the way down the tubes. I knew Jeff was not doing well, but I had to keep my eyes on the Lord, focus on what He has given me, and not give up!

I think the turning point was a year ago when I was in prayer meeting, and God gave me Habakkuk 2:3 (NKJV): "For the vision ... tarries, wait for it." I thought, *Wait a minute, Lord. Why are You giving me that verse now? This is not just any old verse; this is the verse that's been a hallmark—the one You've given me in times of need over the last ten years—it's deeply significant.* Though the vision tarries, I do not give up hope.

Jeff was deeply involved in drug dealing and violence. He robbed a drug dealer, then said, "I have never robbed a good person, Mom." So much for honor among thieves! He said one time, "I'm two different people: I come here Sundays with you, and then I go back to *my* world."

When I got home from a prayer meeting one night, I went into the study and knew, as soon as I looked at my husband, that something was wrong. He said, "Barbara, sit down. I need to talk to you. Jeff has been arrested."

Immediately I thought of that verse in Habakkuk. "Oh, God, You knew what I needed before I knew I needed it." I needed to remember, "Although the vision tarries ... wait for it; it will surely come."

Jeff got out on bail, and he was very shaken up. He knew he was charged with dealing, and he was within two hundred yards of a library, which requires a mandatory sentence of five years. His parking lot was close to the library. He had not been dealing drugs to little kids, but he did involve himself in a deal.

I was angry, not just with Jeff but with the whole situation. Before the trial and sentencing, I sat outside Jeff's house and hugged him. He went into the house, waving at me and crying. He turned around again, smiled, and said, "I'll be okay, Mom. Don't worry about me. I'll be good; I've just got to take my fall."

I got in the car and the cell phone rang; it was a decorator I had contacted earlier, returning my call. *How stupid!* I thought. Who cares what color? Who cares about fabric? Who cares about texture? I cut her short to call friends. I couldn't reach anybody. God said, "I am here. I am here." So I just cried to God and let it rip. I felt better after I got it out.

The night before he was sentenced, Jeff called me. I asked, "Son, how do you want me to pray for you tomorrow?"

"Mom, pray that the judge gives me exactly what I need to turn my life around and not a minute more."

"That's a good prayer, Jeff. I'll pray that."

During his sentencing hearing, Jeff caught my eye. I thought my mother's heart would melt, just melt. He stood so tall and straight in that ugly orange uniform. He had said earlier, "Look for me, Mom. I'll be the only one in orange." He never lost his sense of humor.

They sentenced him to five years with four years suspended; he would do a year in a county jail.

That serious sentence was a turning point. Today he is in an intensive drug-addiction program within the jail. He has been told by those in jail that he's a source of light to the guys. I got a call one night from an inmate imprisoned for computer hacking. He said, "Jeff gave us your number. We lost track of where he was in the jail, and we just wanted to be sure he was doing okay—me and the guys over here in Block B." These are dear men! Later, I wrote them a letter to tell them how I appreciated their call. Jeff said, "Oh, Mom, that makes me proud that you would write to them." I send them little inspirational cards from time to time.

Jeff now goes to chapel. His cell mate, a pharmacist, told me, "I saw this loudmouth punk kid in chapel service and thought, *Who is he?* Two hours later, he was my cell mate. Now we're inseparable. Twenty-three hours a day, he's at my side. I got him doing devotions in the morning and reading the

Bible at night." The pharmacist is now out, but he stays in touch, wanting to know how Jeff is doing.

Jeff is excited and hopeful about the future. He wants to get into business. He said, "Mom, I'm not going to go out and buy a fancy car; I'm going to get a truck with tools. I want to get a used car. I want to invest. I want to make a business for a future. Every night now, Mom, for about a week, I go in my cell, and I get on my hands and knees and pray to God. I thank Him for putting me in this program. I thank Him for letting me come to jail. I needed to come to jail. Chronicle One is over. We are starting Chronicle Two, Mom. It's a new beginning, and I'm going to make it this time. I'm going to make it. Trust me."

On the way to this interview, I thought, *I hope that before this book goes to the publisher, there can be a PS: Jeff is walking straight.* "Though the vision tarries, wait for it." The vision will come to pass. I will stand, because God says the vision will come to pass.

PRESSING ON WITH COURAGE

"For the vision is yet for the appointed time; It hastens toward the goal and it will not fail. Though it tarries, wait for it; For it will certainly come, it will not delay" (Hab. 2:3 NASB). Of all the encouraging verses God has given Barbara, this is the one that stands out. She also felt God gave her another message, and she wasn't so happy to hear it: "I will harden you unto difficulties." She wanted to hear, "It will be okay by six o'clock tonight!" But she understood that God was going to train her for the difficulties she couldn't walk through in her own strength. God says many times in Scripture, "I will give you what you need." (See Isa. 8:11; Matt. 1:8; Rom. 8:32.)

Barbara told me that God showed up frequently in a calendar—one of those little Scripture calendars with a verse for each day of the year in the King James Version. She would put the coffee on every morning, turn that calendar page, and say, "O God, give me something." Her distracted mind couldn't focus on Bible study, but God would meet her in the calendar. She would tape each meaningful entry on the side of the window over her kitchen sink, which eventually was papered with fifteen of the calendar pages, dog-eared and outdated.

"I took Jeff over to those calendar pages by the window when he was high as a kite one night and asked, 'Do you see those promises of God? This is where we're going, son. I don't care what we see right here and now today!' He just hugged me and said, 'I know, Ma.' They looked unsightly on my beautiful peach kitchen wall, but they were precious to me. I couldn't throw them out; it gave me strength to look at them. I recently took them all off the wall to paint and placed them in a shoe box. Someday I'm going to present them to Jeff—probably right before his first evangelistic meeting. Those were God's words to me in that silly, precious little calendar. I truly believed, and I still believe, because I serve a mighty God!"

Barbara's belief has not shielded her from deep anger during her struggles. "There are times when I have been so angry at the Devil. This is a war; it was not over in one battle. And much like when you go to real war, I have had to train myself. It is boot camp. I need to just do it! I need to put one foot in front of the other, and walk—just get through the day, get through the hour, and break it down in small doses."

Jesus said, "My sheep hear me, and they know my voice." (See John 10:27.) Barbara's words remind us to recognize

HE REACHED DOWN FROM ON HIGH AND TOOK HOLD OF ME; HE DREW ME OUT OF DEEP WATERS.

—PSALM 18:16

when God is talking to us and then to listen and obey. That is part of the boot camp experience.

"You have to learn to fight. I've asked God for a warring spirit like Deborah's and for courage. He said, 'Be strong and of good courage. Fear not.' But I have to ask for it. And I realize in my humanity, some days I do better than others."

Barbara has learned it's important to find one good friend you can go to and be honest with. Signs by her telephone prompt her: "Render the throne, not the phone" and "He will not leave you nor forsake you, but that doesn't mean you feel good. It will hurt. The Word is our lifeblood—not family or friends."

I asked Barbara how people make it through deep troubles without the Lord. Says Barbara, "I don't think they do. I have had a counselor listen to my story, just a part of it. Her response was 'You ought to be in an institution; you ought to at least be suffering from a nervous breakdown or be on heavy drugs.' But I haven't had to take those routes, thank the Lord. The Word is my life and my health."

Barbara has learned to keep on keeping on with her life. "In the middle of trouble, we may think, *When this prayer gets answered, then I will do what I'm called to do;* or *When my husband gets saved and this kid gets turned around and the disease goes away, I will do what I'm called to do.* No! Our answer is the here and now, not later.

"I won't even listen to doctrine that says we'll get our reward in the by and by." Barbara is emphatic on this point. "I'm not settling for that. The Lord says He came to give life and give it abundantly. Now. There are some areas that are abundant. There are some areas that are lacking, so I wait until they catch up. I need to live my life now and realize that I will fulfill my call and my destiny in the midst of the pain."

Barbara's story is still unfolding. She recently decided to hang on to a wonderful quote: "Everything will be okay in the end, and if it's not okay, then it ain't the end!"

Is she stubborn? She doesn't know. "I am so determined to see my son serve God. I would like these trials to stop. I've joked, 'To heck with the jewels and the crown! Give me the Burger King crown for now.' I'm tired of working on character, but I can honestly say I'm a better person. I am richer, and in a sense, I am grateful for my experiences. When I see a kid in

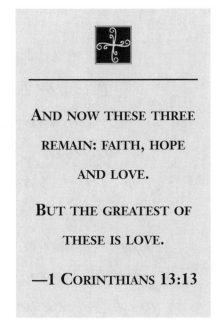

AND NOW THESE THREE REMAIN: FAITH, HOPE AND LOVE.

BUT THE GREATEST OF THESE IS LOVE.

—1 CORINTHIANS 13:13

trouble and I see a mother weeping, I don't judge quickly because of where I've been. I'm not quick to jump to an easy answer. I have more compassion. I am stronger. There are times I've gotten thinner because of all this, so I don't have to diet. These problems take away your appetite real quickly. I wanted Jeff to grow up strong and healthy and loving God. I wanted him to go to college and graduate and get a good job. Is that too much to ask? That doesn't sound too hard. Anyway, isn't that the American dream? So what do I get instead—all the fruits of the Spirit!" At this point the two of us laughed together.

Barbara believes God chose her to be Jeff's mother because He knew she would love Jeff unconditionally and stand on the Word.

"God told me long ago, 'What I whisper to you, you will someday shout from the rooftops.' My 'someday' is coming. It will be worth the wait."

Oswald Chambers said,
"One of the greatest stresses
in life is the stress of waiting
for God." That is why, in the
midst of our struggles and the
apparent lack of progress, we
need to remember that we must
wait, even when success tarries.

—Georgia Shaffer

CHAPTER TWO

Joan: Waiting on God

Joan is a woman who is very graceful and quite lovely. She is tall and thin and regal, and you'd never guess she has lived through so many difficult chapters of life. She is quick to smile and has an easy laugh. Married and a mother of two grown children, Joan is known for her great generosity—giving without keeping accounts.

Her green eyes twinkled as she greeted me in a frequent-flyer lounge at the airport in Seattle. She told me she and her husband live in a small, artsy, terrific home with a grand view of Puget Sound, and she soon told me why we couldn't have our interview there. (My loss—how I love the ocean!) We met to talk about the slice of her life called marriage. Joan immediately said something that truly captured my attention.

"I was so excited about coming here to meet with you. I stopped on the way to get a cup of Starbucks. I walked outside and I noticed how crystal blue the sky was, like the blue sky after a storm clears. I said, 'Oh, I love the sky! I love life! I love people! I love coffee—Starbucks coffee with half-and-half!' I don't care what kind of diet I'm on, I have to have my half-and-half.

"And then I thought, *What am I—crazy? My husband is home*

in bed sleeping off another night of drinking. He's been drinking since I met him and may very well drink until he dies. So what am I so happy about? Yes, my marriage is very difficult and life has lots of troubles, but I still have a spring in my step, and I can truly say I love life. Either I am in very serious denial or I'm a recipient of God's amazing grace (and there are days I wonder which is which)."

"There were seasons when I had toxic faith and plenty of immature denial, but when you do this [a difficult marriage] long enough—after a while you realize that it really *is* God's goodness that pulls you through. That doesn't take away all the hurts. *This is life.* This is my life. This is my marriage. It is hard. God puts the pieces back together and sets you on a path to healing and wholeness."

Joan wasted no time getting down to truth, candor, and the nitty-gritty of her marriage to a "functioning alcoholic." I asked how she could be so painfully honest. She said she hopes the things she shares will help women who need encouragement. Touching just one life through this book would bring her great joy. She explained that she asked the Lord many times to guide her words during the interview. She began to tell her story.

IN HER OWN WORDS: JOAN'S STORY

I was not raised in a vibrant church. I was raised in a dead church. It was a dead mainline church. I'm not being judgmental; *trust me*—it was dead.

I accepted Christ when I was eight years old. There was an evangelist there one Sunday. As clearly as yesterday, I remember her saying, "Who doesn't want to go to hell?" And what eight-year-old wants to go to hell? I raised my hand. But I knew nothing about discipleship, being born anew, or seeking God's plan for my life.

I tried to be good, kind, sweet, and moral, but I really didn't know that I was supposed to ask God who I should marry. I knew enough to quote the verse about not being unequally yoked. I knew when I heard the pure gospel that my religiosity was dead, and there was no life in it. He was not Lord of my life.

So when I met Leo I asked him, "You *do* know Jesus?" Yes, he knew Jesus. "And you *will* go to church?" Yep, he would go to church. I did not have peace about getting married, nor did I have peace the day I walked down the aisle. I cried myself to sleep. I cried on the honeymoon. I knew I was in trouble. That first year of marriage I spent more time crying than all twenty-seven years prior. I was already lonely. I was a virgin when we got married, and I thought, *Oh, good! Now when I get married, this will be great!* Whether it was his depression or the excessive alcohol, I don't know. I thought we could make love every night, maybe two or three times a day! So I felt rejected.

I did everything I could think of. I cooked. I cleaned. I bought all the books. I bought the nightgowns and tried so hard to be a dutiful wife. I tried to be romantic despite his neglect, but I was actually lying down and dying in a negligee. As I mentioned, when I married Leo, I was twenty-seven (so it wasn't that I was some little kid), and he was twenty-nine. It has been hard from day one. There were times I had thoughts like, *Lord, I would have made a pretty good wife! I'm nice. I'm attractive. I'm versatile. What a waste! Lord, yoo-hoo! What about me?* That is just gut honesty. There was real rejection. I knew then and know now at a core level that he loves me, but it's a very fractured love.

After we got married, it was like a light switch flipped. I knew I needed to press into the things of God. I needed a church. I wanted to get into a Bible study and meet Christian friends. I needed to memorize Scripture. And God began to bring me a church, a Christian friend, and a desire to read the Word. I memorized a verse a day, and I would berate myself because I couldn't do more.

Leo never went to church, so I went by myself. I went to every class on children or marriage I could go to. I would hide my Bible because he would get angry. When the kids were born, he let me take them, but he still didn't go. In hindsight, he might have been jealous because I was a "fanatic"—you know, the kind of Christian who should be locked up for a year after meeting Jesus.

I was going to fix him and help him. I never thought about looking at character traits. I know now that he was already an alcoholic. In those days I would have a drink to be social. I would make a pitcher of whiskey sours, and I would sip one while he would finish the pitcher. But I thought, *That's okay, everybody drinks, a lot of nice people get drunk.* So, I guess I had my own cracks.

People tend to think that the alcoholic is the bum in the gutter, but the alcoholic is really the boss at the office or the housewife next door. My husband was thirty. He was making a good living. We had a little house on a wooded acre. It was a nice little beginning; it all looked really good. The alcohol was there before we married. He was moody, so the depression was there too, but I could get him out of it. I could make him laugh. I could nurture him. I was his savior.

One of my "drivers"—the things that motivate me most strongly—is that I am overly responsible. I am not guilty about stuff, but I am overly responsible, which comes from having had older, foreign-born parents and being the only child. When they needed a telephone number, I looked it up because I could spell. I wrote my own note to school when I was sick. I was scared to death the principal would recognize my writing and think we were all lying, even though he knew my parents were foreign and I was writing it. My mother would sign her name. So I was responsible then to help "watch out" for them.

Mother was embarrassed that she would forget how to say the Pledge of Allegiance when she would come to any program at school. I was embarrassed that she couldn't speak English like other parents. I remember coming home from being with a friend's family one day and my mother had written a note so I would know where she was, and it said "Went to bich" [beach]. I was embarrassed and afraid someone would think my mother was cursing. I've since learned that was a problem called *shame*. I probably could have been an alcoholic if God hadn't intervened. It was one of the few things in life where I knew God said, "Stop!" He knew where I was going—and it certainly would have been a quick fix in life.

I don't know what it is to be nurtured in that truest sense. I didn't get something I should have gotten and should still get—this *nurture*. It hurts. So I tell the Lord, "I know where I am without You. I would be a mess without You." Without the Lord I would have left long ago, looking for another Prince Charming. I probably would have ended up in another alcoholic marriage.

I think what attracted me to my husband is that chemistry that draws the unhealthy part of me and the unhealthy part of him together. I was drawn to him because I was going to fix him, and he needed me in order to function. Also, he is very ADD, and I am very organized and detailed and can do things he cannot. I'm good with people. He's not. He would say that opposites attract, and I thought that was so wonderful. Now I realize how sick it was. He would say, "I need you,"

and that just played into that part of me that is overly responsible and broken.

Love is blind. When I say I loved him, I don't believe it
was true love; I believe it was loneliness, neediness, and lust.
It was definitely a needy love. At age twenty-seven, I was getting the question, "How come you're not married?" And I
didn't date a lot. I was tall and there weren't many tall guys.
He was tall, six feet four inches, had the same ethnic back-
ground, and owned his own business. Besides, he could
provide for me.

The great things about Leo … well, under the brusqueness,
he has a tender heart. There is not a greedy bone in his body.
He is very giving. Sometimes it was for the wrong reasons,
but even still, giving—he's just not greedy. And he loves animals. That's one of the things I loved about him. He had two
big dogs when I met him.

What else did I fall in love with? His cleverness, intelli-
gence, tenaciousness. When we did make love, I used to tell
myself, *It may not be quantity, but it is quality.* There was no
problem with it when it happened, it was just that it hardly
ever happened. What did I fall in love with? I often ask
myself that question. I can't say I'm in love with him now. He
doesn't make my heart pitter patter. Most of my life for the
last ten years has been a conscious effort to stay in the marriage. I'm there because I came into covenant, and God has
not told me to go. My dear mother, at age ninety-one, said to
me, "I don't know how you have stood it so long." (She
hasn't seen the half of it.) My mother didn't come from a
generation where women left their husbands. My father was
not easy either.

Leo is very clever. His mind is good, bright, intelligent, far superior to mine. I always say, "I'm sweet; he's intelligent." Not much of a sense of humor, but he is very creative and entrepreneurial. He is strong-willed and tenacious. He holds on to a fault like a bulldog, but it can also be a positive. He loves the sea. I think that was attractive to me because I, too, love the ocean.

Despite not being "in love" with him, I do have feelings for him. The time he had serious chest pain and was in the hospital, my heart ached for him. I look at him with pity sometimes, which is not a good way to look at a mate. But that is the truth. Some days I love my dog more. Dog lovers will understand that. (Seriously though, people should live as well as my dog.) Maybe I view him as a brother; I would not choose him as a friend. Yes, a brother—not a friend. I don't really trust him. He might not hurt me physically or by closing a checking account, but I can't trust that if I say something, it won't come out somewhere else. Through alcoholic arguments there have been times he has said very hurtful things, very hurtful! As much as I have done the inner healing, the counseling, even now, painful memories come up as I'm talking. Some things are hard to let go of. As far as we've (Christians) come as believers, we still have a way to go. *Nobody* has fully arrived.

I can say that for thirty-one years it's been hard. In the process I have changed; he has mellowed. But it's been hard. On the honeymoon it was more that I was disappointed. It was probably very selfish. I wanted to make love more and go out, and he would sleep in. There was just no response. So from that standpoint, maybe I was selfish, I don't know. But I don't think I realized the severity of the drinking problem until we were married a year or two. We would go into town and see friends, and they would all get drunk, and he would drink until he almost passed out.

Several years ago, someone told me I needed to go Alcoholics Annonymous (AA) meetings. I needed to deal with the alcoholism. There were times, for example, when I was pregnant—this is one of those stories that I guess I haven't dealt with yet because it still comes up very readily. I was pregnant with Alice, our second child, due very soon, and I begged Leo not to drink because I thought I might go into labor. He went ahead and drank. I remember crying, "If I go into labor tonight, who will take me?" I don't know if he had passed out, but he wasn't going to drive me to the hospital.

> NOW IS YOUR TIME OF GRIEF, BUT I WILL SEE YOU AGAIN AND YOU WILL REJOICE, AND NO ONE WILL TAKE AWAY YOUR JOY.
>
> —JOHN 16:22

Another time, when Alice was an infant, I had the flu. I woke him up because I was going to throw up, and said, "Alice is crying." No response. I walked to her crib, and I remember swallowing the vomit so I didn't throw up on her as I was picking her up. And then I lay on the floor in her room and just wept. I had a pity party. And that is a hard one to let go. There are lots of memories like that.

I know abandonment, yes. Emotional abandonment. What is the difference between being physically abused or emotionally abused? The pain is real.

One of the characteristics of an alcoholic is personality

change. They are happy-go-lucky guys when they drink, generally speaking. The guy who is uptight and tense, after a few drinks becomes Mr. Nice Guy, happy and silly. And that was Leo. He was normally tense and uptight, but when he drank he was kind of silly. Now, he could get mean, but basically, he was not a mean drunk. He could get angry, but he wasn't throwing things against the wall.

Leo never hit me, though he shoved me a couple of times. I don't remember that as much as the verbal abuse. It was more that he quietly drank himself to sleep in the chair. With the kids, Dad was just not there. He was physically there but not emotionally there.

Alcoholism and the Children
In regard to the children, I learned that I had to tell the truth but not a whole lot of gory details. Children need to hear, "Daddy is sick" or "Daddy has a problem," but not "Daddy is a no-good bum and he's drunk." Maybe you say, "Daddy drank too much." There needs to be truth, or you produce children who don't trust their instincts because they can't feel safe with those they are supposed to trust.

Leo would come home with a twelve pack, and it would be a twelve pack every night. He stopped the hard liquor because that just wiped him out too much, so he would drink beer. We had volumes of trash. Living out in the country, we didn't have trash pickup; we had to take it down to the main road ourselves. So the kids in the area would see large bags and cartons full of beer bottles. Scott, our son, would throw the beer cans into the woods. I didn't know until two years later, but the young boy down the street would come up and tease Scott and Alice about all the beers their dad drank, because he would see all the beer cans and the beer bottles.

We would try to make a family night and do a special

something—a special meal in the dining room, a special dessert. But Leo would never make it to the family night, and there was such an obvious void. When you're married with kids, you can't have family night without Dad. It was just one night that I asked that he be there, and he wouldn't get there. And it wasn't because he was busy with work. He had generally gone to the local pub for a few beers. So they didn't see their dad much.

My thirty-seventh birthday fell on family night, and Leo didn't make it. I cried; I wept. But I had the kids. I still have the card the kids made me after they realized their dad wasn't showing up. They grieved for me, so it polarized their emotions. They were angry at their dad for what he did to their mom, and yet, thank God, I had good teaching and counsel not to badmouth Leo. They instinctively saw what they saw. A counselor told me, "Do not take responsibility for what the alcoholism has done." Those are wise words because my tendency was to be a responsible person and therefore to take responsibility for a lot of it. I realized I didn't always have to take the blame; it was the alcoholism.

I was grateful that Leo did let me teach the children about God and take them to church. I knew some women at the time who were not allowed to read the Bible to their kids. So I was blessed in that sense, but they did not see their daddy go to church except maybe Easter and Christmas. My son used to be so afraid to go to church. He would say, "Mom, I'm afraid when we walk in, they'll think you're divorced." They went through a time when they both were afraid that we would get divorced. I think most kids go through that. Our situation planted many fears in them. My heart hurts about that, but I trust the Great Healer.

I was basically a single parent. I didn't want to hand off the ball at night to my husband. He was not receiving, and I didn't even want to hand off the ball because he would drop it as a result of drinking. I did all the chauffeuring, counseling, cheering, and nursing.

It was rare that we went out and did anything. Most of our friends were my friends. There are some friends who have said, "It's just because of Leo we don't want to go to dinner. We love you, but it's painful. It's too hard."

First Steps toward Healing and Understanding

I started by going to counseling. A wise pastor-friend said, "Let's make sure we're doing all we can do for the children. I want you to see a counselor." So I did, after I had been to AA a while. I can remember saying to Leo, "I'm going to an AA meeting," and he would refuse to watch Alice for me because she was a baby. So I would have to take Alice to a babysitter. I have one vivid memory: It was pouring rain. I thought I would take Alice to a babysitter at night, go to AA, go back to the babysitter, and then I would go home. And of course, he was` drunk and angry because I went to AA.

I SOUGHT THE LORD, AND HE ANSWERED ME; HE DELIVERED ME FROM ALL MY FEARS. THOSE WHO LOOK TO HIM ARE RADIANT; THEIR FACES ARE NEVER COVERED WITH SHAME.

—PSALM 34:4–5

When I went to counseling, he would refuse to pay for it. I was getting healthy, so I said, "Well, I'll get a job to pay for it." The jig was up. You can think you're a social drinker, but when your wife has gone off to AA, something is wrong somewhere. "I went to AA," I told him, "because I need help to learn how to live in this situation."

Later on—after counseling—I did an intervention. We had been sailing on the Fourth of July. We were in the Pacific, and that day everybody was drunk except me and the kids. It was disgusting. I remember thinking, *Enough is enough. I'm doing an intervention. I'm doing something. I could live like this forever, but I do not want this to destroy my children.* That mother's heart just rises up like a lion, and you are going to fight for your cubs. Scott was already throwing the beers and acting out, and he hated that his dad drank. He would pray, "God, help Daddy with the drinking." Alice was having nervous ticks that I believe were symptomatic of the stress in the home.

I went to an intervention counselor and went through the process. We had people in our home and surprised Leo and told him he was an alcoholic. That's when I said, "If you do not get help"—I didn't have the guts to say, "I will leave," which is what they wanted me to say—not a divorce, but separation. I left for twenty-four hours and came back, and he stopped drinking for a year. He refused drink.

Now he was a "dry drunk." He had all the behaviors of alcoholism: the irritability, the control, the anger. But we didn't have the drinking, which helped. He said he could see clearly for the first time in a long time. He recognized differences—yet he was a dry drunk with white knuckles. He knew he would go back to it sometime. He was showing me that he could stop because he didn't want to lose his family.

In all those years of drinking, Leo would go late to work because he was hung over. When you're a boss and own your own business, you can pretty much make your own hours.

He worked late a lot. His dad had taught him that the business comes first. We were married a month, and Leo went off to trade conferences and conventions. A month, and I barely heard from him. That has been a subtle theme through our married life. The "almighty business" was his god. Leo has since realized how empty that is.

I'm thankful that Leo has always wanted me to be provided for, to be taken care of. I've heard horror stories of women who are told by their husbands, "You are on your own. Too bad!" Leo really wants to make sure everything is okay—should he go before me—business, money, whatever. That is a blessing.

Pressing on in Spite of the Pain

Sometimes I would call my best friend, Linda, who has a beautiful marriage. "I need a reality check because it's hard for me to know what is reality. Is it normal that you would want to look for something good in your husband? Is it normal to crave affection?" That kind of thing. I often don't know *normal*. To Leo, I would say [or think], "Is it too much to expect that I would want you to put your arms around me when you just found out your dad died instead of barking at me that he's dead? Am I expecting too much?" For that kind of reality check, I would go to her because she does have a nurturing relationship.

My hands were covered with eczema during the season I went to AA. As you know, adrenals equip us for "fight or flight." In fright your adrenaline kicks in, and your adrenals start putting out: when the dinner burns, the dog throws up, the baby is crying—just the daily stresses of life. It's those daily things compounded that produce cortisol, and I had such constant daily stress that I had eczema. I had finally gone to a homeopathic doctor, who diagnosed it as such. If I put on cortisone to help it, it would become even worse.

TRUST IN THE LORD WITH ALL YOUR HEART AND LEAN NOT ON YOUR OWN UNDERSTANDING.

—PROVERBS 3:5

My hands were raw. They looked like I had been in a fire. They were blistered; they itched. I put them in hot water to stop the itch. The dermatologist said, "Keep your hands out of water." I said, "I have babies! What do you mean, keep my hands out of water?" He said, "Take an art class." I took a painting class to try to do something for myself to alleviate the stress that was causing my eczema.

I begged God to heal my hands, because I couldn't function. I was sitting at an Episcopal healing service when God said, "I am going to heal you inside out." As I went to counseling and to AA and got out all my stuffed-down feelings, my hands began to heal. Leo said, "I guess it's all worth it, if you go to counseling for your hands to be healed." He could see the difference.

I used that story of my hands to teach my daughter when she had a lot of anxiety. "Alice, you need to get it out. Remember Mommy's hands. If you don't get it out and talk about it, it makes you sick inside. So we have to get these thoughts out, whether it is to Mom or a trusted friend. You need to talk about it and tell God."

Yes, number one, you have to recognize you have stress and not pretend everything is okay. How do I deal with stress? I self-talk. There is a fine line between that talk and faith. I am real with God. "I can do all things through Christ who strengthens me" (Phil. 4:13 NASB).

A counselor I knew back then said to me recently, "You did make the right choice. I used to think you should leave." Many counselors have told me to leave Leo, but this counselor has come back to me now and said, "You made the harder choice." The secular counselor will say, "Pick up your bags, baby. The plane is waiting. Don't look back. You deserve better! Go!" Friends may say the same. But I cannot say I altruistically stayed for the cause. I think I stayed out of fear. I'm not sure I stayed because it is where God wanted me. I would like to think of it this way, that He never told me to leave—and I do hear from God. I would like to think He would have made it clearer if I was supposed to go, but I don't know that.

You know I really thought … I thought my life would be like *The Donna Reed Show*. Maybe that's why I still wear pearls. Remember Donna Reed? I couldn't get past the pearls, and the dad was always right there. I really thought our family would be like Donna Reed's. I thought we would love God and serve God and open our home to friends. I didn't ask for a whole lot. I don't know that I had any dreams beyond being a mom, and I wanted to serve God. I wondered, *God, is that such a big deal?* I didn't think I would walk alone as long as I have. Thank God, I didn't know thirty-one years ago that thirty-one years later I would still be so alone in my marriage. God is wise. I never dreamt it would go on this long. Even when I say that, though, somewhere deep inside I do have hope. Sometimes it's barely detectable, but it's there. God is alive—and so is my hope.

THEREFORE PUT ON THE FULL ARMOR OF GOD, SO THAT WHEN THE DAY OF EVIL COMES, YOU MAY BE ABLE TO STAND YOUR GROUND, AND AFTER YOU HAVE DONE EVERYTHING, TO STAND.

—EPHESIANS 6:13

I heard from God, "I am the I AM. Press on. Press in." For the longest time all I kept hearing in my spirit was "Press." That is not exactly what you want to hear when you say, "God, speak to me. I'm tired. I'm weary in my heart and my bones." But it is what I needed to do, to press, to push, to stand. In the midst of it, He has met me at every turn, granted strength for the day, and even given me a sense of humor. And who doesn't need a good laugh?

When you have put it all on [the armor of God], and you have prayed your heart out, and you have fasted your gut out, there is not a whole lot left to do but *stand*. And it is all about timing and seasons. Through the years and the tears I've learned that I've just got to stand. I don't have to do it well—I learned that too. I just have to stand.

Now, when you are not pressing, you are standing. But I guess they are really intertwined. Pressing sounds more active, but there are times that the pressing is emotional rather than physical. I have to keep on keeping on. It's a decision; it's a choice. It's okay to fall apart in the midst of it, but then you get back up. It's the "I fall down, I get up; I fall down, I get up" approach to life.

Devotion in the Desert

I'm reminded of a book that I read years ago that was called *Beloved Unbeliever* [Berry, Zondervan, 1981]. There is a danger when you have a husband who isn't committed to God or doesn't walk like you think he should. The danger is to begin to believe that he is less than human—and certainly not as good as the Christian men in church. I have had to learn to love my husband right where he is. I am his wife, and whether or not he meets every expectation, I am accountable to God's directive for a wife to love her husband, regardless of whether he is saved, sanctified, or set free.

Leo is an alcoholic and he battles depression, but I have never felt released from my covenant with him. I'm not saying I have everything mastered, but it is my goal to be more like Jesus. Consequently, I am very comfortable (in the right sense) with unbelievers. It doesn't derail me when someone cusses or shares a messy secret. Much of our married life has been sporadically spent with some of his friends who aren't believers, and it has enriched me to not have every little duck in a row. I desperately try to not change Leo. I ask God most days, "God, make me the wife that Leo needs. Help me not to focus on his shortcomings, Lord—just change me. Please change me. Do something so that this marriage can be redeemed." The hope for Leo to change is not always strong, but there is always some hope that God will turn things around. Of late I have come to the realization that hope is all I have on the hard days.

It seems impossible not to compare our marriage to others. It's painful to sit in church and see a couple put their arms around one another. It's hard to see nurturing. I feel lonely. It's been very painful, and I was surprised by my emotions during my daughter's courtship and wedding. Those feelings dropped out of nowhere and I felt privately embarrassed. The flowers, the cards, the tenderness—it all magnifies my lack. I

> ONE THING I ASK OF THE LORD, THIS IS WHAT I SEEK: THAT I MAY DWELL IN THE HOUSE OF THE LORD ALL THE DAYS OF MY LIFE, TO GAZE UPON THE BEAUTY OF THE LORD AND TO SEEK HIM IN HIS TEMPLE.
>
> —PSALM 27:4

don't want to be jaded in any way, but it is very painful. There again, I think, *Darn you, Satan, here's yet another thing you're trying to rob me of.* I don't want to miss any of the normal joys of my daughter falling in love and getting married. Waiting is hard. I am not in denial about it. I recognize all the danger signs and the need to stay close to the Lord.

When I take control and ignore the Holy Spirit, that's the thing that gets me into trouble and makes me fret. If I could have taken God's hand more often and sat down more and trusted Him in the big and small things, I would have saved myself a lot of sleepless nights.

When a person starts going to AA meetings, they may continue drinking, but they won't ever again drink the same way. Alcoholics know they should not take a drink. They learn boundaries and disciplines. It's the same thing with God: Once you are aware of Him, once you attend some meetings, once you meet others with the same goals, you are never the same. The Holy Spirit pricks my heart and He makes me aware: "Joan, you're getting into self-pity, stop it and move on! You have so much to be grateful for." And I really do—but I have to purpose in my heart to look *above* the circumstances.

My view of God has definitely changed over the years. He is so much bigger than I thought. He really doesn't need me. He truly is all sufficient. When I say, "God, tell me something this morning," He says, "I AM that I am." Where do you go after that? What have I learned about Jesus? I see Him, not only holding my hand in a victory parade, but also carrying me above the ashes. When I accepted Christ as that little eight-year-old girl, I didn't want to go to hell. That's not a great reason to get right with God, but it helps. I was looking to the end, and I had never realized He would be going with me to the end and, yes, even right into eternity. I am in awe of God for coming in the heat, in the midst, in the thick of our trouble. He's been with me all the time, and He always will. He is right with me.

THOSE WHO WAIT ON THE LORD SHALL RENEW THEIR STRENGTH; THEY SHALL MOUNT UP WITH WINGS LIKE EAGLES, THEY SHALL RUN AND NOT BE WEARY, THEY SHALL WALK AND NOT FAINT.

—ISAIAH 40:31 (NKJV)

For those who are walking through the desert, on a long, lonely journey, it helps to remember that we are not alone. In truth, God is with us all the time. What a relief.

There seems to be something
that the desert alone can gift us
with. Perhaps it's because there
are no other distractions.
Perhaps it's the very aloneness,
the silence, that makes us finally
listen to all the rumblings in
our souls.

—Sheila Walsh

CHAPTER THREE

Maria:
Holding the Lord's Hand

When I pulled into Maria's driveway, I must admit it felt like home. Not my home, but more like my grandmother's home or the homes of relatives where we used to spend Sundays and holidays when I was a child.

Maria was waiting at the mailbox at the end of her very short driveway, and as we hugged on the front stoop, the familiar smells of "real" Italian cooking wafted through the screen door. Her almost-fifty-year-old, modest, two-bedroom ranch sat on a neat, tree-lined street in a middle-class neighborhood in northern New Jersey, not far from Manhattan.

Short and full-figured with wavy white hair, Maria is a high-energy, sharp-witted septuagenarian. She speaks at a fast "northern" pace and with a clearly audible volume. Her hands and her eyes communicate as colorfully as her words. I first met Maria at a women's event a year earlier and was sure we would meet again. In our brief first encounter, I was struck by her deep joy, her big faith, her vast knowledge of Scripture, and her exuberant love for God in the midst of numerous battles with cancer.

Little did I know at the time that the cancer was only the tip of the iceberg—or shall I say, "the continental glacier"? Maria has had trouble in her life. Lots of trouble. Her theme song could easily be "Nobody Knows the Trouble I've Seen."

Lunch was stupendous, and I was tempted to take a nap but fought off the urge. We settled into her small living room, and I sank into the couch as she got comfortable in her recliner. We prayed, and then she enthusiastically commenced the interview without my having posed the first question: "My life reads like a bad 'B' movie!"

I couldn't wait to hear her explanation.

IN HER OWN WORDS: MARIA'S STORY

Sometimes I hesitate to tell people about all the things that have happened in my life because it almost reads like the script for a grade-B movie. People say, "Oh, it's impossible for that many things to have happened to one person and for you to still be sane." I don't know how sane I really am, but the fact is, I've been able to have a strong mind and a strong faith and a sense of humor in spite of the things that have gone on in my life.

In *my* movie (unlike in an "A" movie), it hasn't all worked out in the end. Thankfully, I go back to the Word because *He* is the Beginning and the End, and it is *His* grace, love, and strength that make everything truly work out in the end. On the very last page in my Bible I have drawn a smiley face with the words "We win!!!" There are exclamation points because sometimes I have had to turn to that page in need of hope and to be reminded of God's promises. There are times when all our theological theories are replaced by a feeling of having been betrayed, not only by life, but by God Himself. Occasionally, I have had to turn to the back of the Bible just to remind myself that we really do win in the end. In the meantime, there are many lessons and many things to work through.

I grew up in an abusive family. It was an abusive childhood—physically, verbally, psychologically—the whole thing goes together. I learned that I had to be totally self-sufficient, but my self-esteem was low. That's why I was ripe to enter an abusive marriage where, again, I had to be totally self-sufficient. My self-reliance was good in some ways because it sustained me, but on the negative side, the Devil used my innate strength plus my self-sufficiency, which equaled a well-disguised pride. I was self-sufficient unto myself but not unto God.

I went from an abusive mother and father to an abusive husband. I married Albert because he seemed to be a good man. From our first date until the day we got married, only six months elapsed. I couldn't have known in that short time that he was mentally ill.

Yes, I married a stranger. We got along very well while we dated. Albert was big and handsome, and I wanted to belong to someone because my childhood and growing years had been filled with sadness and rejection. I married in 1960; back in those days you didn't think about a man's friends or whether he had a mentor. Most of his friends were married. He had just gotten out of the army and was looking to get married. He seemed like a good guy. He hung around with some of my friends who had gone to school with him. He was from a fairly nice Italian family. What more was there?

I got pregnant right away when we got married. The first

slap was about six months into the marriage. When our first child was born, she didn't sleep through the night for a year and had some minor health complications. During that time the abuse worsened quickly. It was terrible. My nose has been broken so many times, it is a wonder it's still straight. I'm a survivor.

I would go to court and get a court order for protection, and then he would say to me, "You think that piece of paper is going to keep me away from you? If I want to see you, or I want to be here, they'll have to put a bullet through my heart, and I will still see you. When you least expect it, I will be there, and I will kill you! Because if I can't live with you, I'm not going to live without you." And I believed him.

Because I had been physically abused in my childhood, I had that "suffering is normal" mentality. I used to think some people were meant to be happy, some people were meant to suffer, and I was one of the latter. That was my lot in life. That is what God had chosen for me, and I would pray to accept my lot in life, not knowing I didn't have to. That makes me so sad now. It makes me very sad. God said, "My people perish for lack of knowledge" (see Job 36:12). Without Scripture and a devotion to God, we're very lost.

I was stuck in a vicious cycle. Albert would say, "I wish I could cut my hands off. I will never do it again. I love you." He would be so good, good, good. He really loved me to the nth degree. I mean "out there" when he talked about me, I was the greatest. I was the great economizer. I was the greatest cook. I was this; I was that. But, definitely, there was something in him that hated me to the same degree that he loved me. When he was unbalanced and plagued, he acted it out.

There were times I had to be hospitalized. The police would come to the house, see me bloody, and say, "Oh, this is domestic. We don't get involved in domestic stuff," and they would walk out again. They wouldn't do anything. Even when the neighbors would call the police, the police would just say, "This is a domestic thing. We don't get involved."

With women's lib, I was finally getting a sense of who I was. I suddenly decided that I didn't have to put up with this anymore.

There was an incident when we were eating supper, and I said something to Albert that got him angry. I had just served him a cup of tea, and he took the cup of boiling hot tea and threw it at me. Some of it splashed and hit little Annie (our daughter) on the shoulder. Of course, she screamed in pain. So he jumped up and said to me, "You better get out of the house because today I am going to kill you. *Today* I am going to kill you."

He got the ice cubes and was putting them on her arm. I was outside the house crouching behind my garbage pails, and I said, "Oh, my God, my father is going to get me. Oh, my God, my father is going to get me." Then I thought, *My father is going to get me? I am back hiding from my father again. I am forty-one years old and I am still hiding from my father.*

I concluded that I may as well have been dead. It was not the way to live. I went back in the house, and Albert said, "I told you not to set foot in this house because I am going to kill you."

I said, "Well, I *am* in the house, and you better kill me. Let me tell you something. If you kill me today, you know what is going to happen to you?" (He was president of the Lion's Club. He was on the Zoning Board of Appeals here in the county. It was his aspiration to be in politics. Big mucky-muck, right?) I said, "Let me tell you what will happen if you kill me.

If you kill me, you are going to lose me, you are going to lose your children. You are going to lose this house, and more than anything else, you are going to lose your good name.

> I LIE DOWN AND SLEEP; I WAKE AGAIN, BECAUSE THE LORD SUSTAINS ME.
>
> —PSALM 3:5

"If you hit me and you don't kill me, let me tell you what is going to happen. You are going to lose me, you are going to lose your house, and you are going to lose your children. And if I have to sell my own body, I will take out a full-page ad in the local paper, and I will record every broken bone, every internal bleeding, every hospitalization, everything you have ever done to me, and I will have in big headlines: *The Great Albert* _____ *Is a Wife Beater.* I will have *all* the facts there to back it up."

He stopped in his tracks, looked at me, and said, "You know, *you* are crazy!"

I said, "I *am* crazy, I *am* crazy!" The victim now became the abuser. I looked at him and I saw fear in his eyes. He was huge. I mean he was huge; he wore a size 54 jacket, a big man physically. I said to him, "You know what else? You will never, ever have another night's sleep for the rest of your life, because when you least expect it, I am going to take a knife and I am going to cut that big fat stomach out, and I am going to step over your bloody body, and then I am going to go to the movies."

And he said to me, "You ARE crazy!"

"I said, You are RIGHT. I *am* crazy! You know what? For the first time in my life, I am actually sane. I have been crazy all along, and now I am finally sane. You will *never* hit me again."

And he never did.

Not that the abuse stopped. His mental illness worsened, and he tried to kill me several times. Once he wrapped ropes around my neck trying to hang me from the ceiling fixture. By then he had lost touch with reality and got it into his head that I was a spy with the Greek government. He was the 007 agent who had been assigned to find the master spies. And that was me, the master spy.

Back then his illness was thought to be full-blown schizophrenia. I'm not sure if that's what he really had, but he was definately crazy—a very sick soul.

I was raised a Catholic, and I was a good girl. I went to mass growing up and continued even when I worked on Wall Street. There was a church right around the corner on Wall Street, so I went to mass almost every day on my lunch hour.

I prayed a lot. Even after I was married, when my daughter Annie was sick, I would pray. It was my mentality to be accepting of suffering, and I was more into tradition and ritual rather than a relationship with God. It wasn't really until I got saved that my love for God was birthed, more than twenty years ago.

When I first gave my heart to Jesus, somebody gave me a tape with this note: "Congratulations on your commitment to Christ; here is a wonderful tape!" One of the songs on it had these lyrics:

> At the cross, at the cross where I first saw the light,
>   and the burden of my sin rolled away;
> It was there by faith, I received my sight,
>   and now I am happy all the day!

Well, how many times was I tempted to rip up that tape! What kind of idiot is "happy all the day"? I found God, but I was far from "happy all the day."

THIS IS WHAT THE LORD SAYS: STAND AT THE CROSSROADS AND LOOK; ASK FOR THE ANCIENT PATHS, ASK WHERE THE GOOD WAY IS, AND WALK IN IT, AND YOU WILL FIND REST FOR YOUR SOULS.

—JEREMIAH 6:16

Some people think Christianity is a panacea: *Oh, once you get saved, everything is going to be wonderful! You will see your whole life change!* Well, your whole life doesn't change because the troubles of this world keep coming. What changes is that you get through trials with peace, knowing that Somebody is there with you. But we are not saved from pain. Oh yes, in the beginning there is the honeymoon, like every marriage, and then the work starts. At first everything you pray for gets answered. Praying is a joy. Then after a while the work starts. You say, "You know what, my prayers aren't being answered as quickly as they were before."

When I got saved, I was like a drowning person gulping a breath of fresh air. I remember we were in the process of a divorce. We never did get divorced, but we were going through divorce proceedings. I had gone to this non-Catholic church, and they were having a three-day revival. The revival lasted for thirty-nine days. I was there for thirty-six of the thirty-nine days (for evening services). Albert had said to me one night, "Do you mind telling me where you're going every night?"

I said, "We are no longer in a position that I have to answer to you. But so your mind doesn't travel where it shouldn't be, I am going to church."

"What church has meetings every night until 10:30 or 11:00?"

I said, "I am not going to Saint Anthony's; I am going to a born-again church."

So he called the priest and reported me, and the priest called me. "Maria, what is this I hear?"

I said, "Father, I have been slowly starving to death—in the church and in my marriage. For the first time in my life, I am being fed in a way that I have never been fed before." It was because of that Word of God, which at first I could not believe was even relevant, but there was so much there for me. Then, of course, I kept searching the Bible, and that is why ultimately I never went through with the divorce. I could find nothing in the Bible to justify divorce. I should have left, but there was really nothing to justify divorce except adultery, and that was not the situation for either one of us.

Tragically, I thought the beatings were normal. Forty or fifty years ago, there was no counseling or support for domestic violence. A woman didn't go to the social worker because she didn't know one existed—and if they did exist, they were rare. I was caught in a vicious and demoralizing cycle that we are now all too familiar with. The perpetrator continues to apologize and promise it will never happen again.

But when my husband started hitting Annie, I knew the marriage had to end. The first time he hit her hard, blood came out of her nose, so I called the police and had him arrested. What I never did for myself, I did for Annie. I said to him, "I will slam you into jail any time you step out of line. If you want nothing more than to be in local politics, your days are over." The fear of being found out was enough to keep him in control—for a while.

I knew I had the right to leave him, and I really wanted it to be totally over. I wanted no part of this man; his illness was progressing rapidly. Eventually, I worked up the courage to pursue a divorce. Then the night before we were signing the final divorce papers, he got saved!

I was fifty-one years old, and my daughter Annie, who was now a woman, had to move back in with her two little ones after her divorce and serious financial and physical problems. I got saved the same year my first grandchild was born. Albert could see the difference in my life. I was kinder, gentler, more patient, and I controlled my sharp tongue.

I was saying, "Oh God, You've got *some* sense of humor! God, if You don't want me to go through this, You will have to let me know, but God, please, *please* let the divorce go through!"

Here's what happened: I had hung a flyer on the refrigerator (as a reminder to myself) announcing that *the* Lauren Chapin, who played the daughter on *Father Knows Best*, was coming to speak at my church. Albert was a movie buff and TV addict. He asked, "What is Lauren Chapin doing going to your church?"

I answered, "She was a heroin addict and was sent to prison and now has a full-time ministry. She travels the country preaching the Word of God."

The next morning he said to me, "What time is your service?"

"Why do you want to know?"

"Well, because I thought I might go and listen to her."

I thought, *I don't want him coming to my church. (Lord, forgive me)*. The next morning I was tiptoeing around the house because I didn't want him to know I was up; I wanted to get out of the house before he woke up. I went into the kitchen, and he was sitting there all showered, shaved, and dressed. I was so angry.

"Do you want to go to church?" he asked.

"No, I don't want to go to church with *you*." We weren't even talking. We were supposed to sign the divorce papers the next day—and he had to go and get saved!

I was miffed, I tell you. I was miffed with God. "God, don't bring him around now!" I wanted him out of my life. At that point, I didn't hate him anymore. I actually felt nothing for him. I had no feelings whatsoever. I didn't hate him; I didn't *anything* him. That is really the opposite of love, by the way, not having any feelings for anybody. Hatred means you are really tied in with very strong love and disappointment in the person you still have such deep feelings for. But you are so hurt you hate them. I didn't feel anything.

So we both went to church that morning, and Lauren Chapin was going on and on and on. At the end of the service, the pastor asked, "Anybody want to come up for prayer?"

Albert shot straight up for prayer. I thought, *Oh, God, what are you doing?*

Afterward, we went home. I was invited to a twenty-fifth anniversary party for some church friends, and, as usual, I went alone. Albert showed up at the same party, and then Lauren Chapin showed up. She said to Pastor, "I never gave my testimony; can I come back tonight, Pastor?" Pastor happily announced that everybody should come back at 7:00 that night.

So I am at this anniversary party on a Sunday afternoon, and to make a long story short, Albert and I both went back to church together. My church friends looked at me curiously, knowing we were getting divorced the next day. I said, "What are you looking at *me* for? *I* don't know what's going on."

That night when Lauren asked if anybody wanted to pray, Albert shot straight up again. He had gone up in the morning and was prayed over, and that night he gave his heart to the Lord. Later that night, he knocked at the door of my bedroom and asked, "If I'm willing to go for counseling, would you consider not signing the papers tomorrow morning?"

I had been praying, "God, if You don't want me to go through with this divorce, You have to let me know, with no doubts. You have to intervene." And then when He intervened, I am telling you, I was so upset! "Oh God, how could you? Please tell me this is not the answer! Oh God, I want him out of my life." But it didn't work out that way.

Talk about a dilemma. I was praying, "God, let Thy will be done!" And then He told me what He wanted—and I was miffed! But I never divorced Albert.

Even though he was saved, Albert was still under the grip of his mental illness. Only a few people knew how sick he was— mainly my pastor and his wife. Not the whole church, but just certain people in the church who, several times, had to come and rescue me because Albert had boarded up all the windows and the doors and pulled out all the phone lines. When things went too far, I actually broke a window and got out of the house. I got crisis intervention to come. They took him away the first time. Then the second time was about a year later. At the time he died, he was heading for another breakdown.

The day he died, Albert called and said, "Maria, I am going to the hospital."

I said, "You're in pain, aren't you?"

He said, "Yes, I really am. Kiss the girls for me. I have to tell you something—you are a real pain, but I need you to know I love you."

I said, "I love you, too, Albert."

He said, "But I love Jesus more!"

"If you are going to the hospital, I will meet you there."

"No, don't go there. I will be okay. I love you." As he hung up the phone, he dropped it. Those were the last words out of his mouth. The rescue squad came and took him to the hospital. They did get his heart beating, but he never started breathing again. He died of a heart attack. He was young. He was fifty-six when he died.

When my husband died, we were providing for our debilitated (single) daughter and two grandchildren. Albert had cashed in his life insurance policy one week before he died, so there was no life insurance. We didn't have two dimes to rub together. I was just recuperating from major surgery—my first cancer operation. Humanly speaking, he couldn't have died at a worse time.

I remember being in the hospital emergency waiting room when the nurse came in and gave me his wedding band and his wallet. She said, "Sorry," and just walked out of the room. I looked up toward heaven and cried, "God, what could You be thinking about? What could You be thinking about, God? You know I need him. I am not strong enough. I need him, and we have Annie and the children to take care of, and I am still in a lot of pain from the surgery, and we have no money; there is no insurance."

All of a sudden I stopped and said, "Wait a minute, wait a minute, God. You know everything. You who made the heavens and the earth, You who sustain all things by the word of Your power and the power of Your Word, You know what I need, but I'm telling You my situation as though You don't know!" Then I said, "God, if You know all these things, then that must mean You are going to take care of us. And You *better*, God! Please—You better, God!"

I always say, you don't mess with God; you don't give Him orders because we are not in a position to do that. I said to the Lord, "If I don't have You, I don't have anything." That was the sinking into the storm, the sinking into the waves, saying, *Save*

MY GOD WILL MEET ALL YOUR NEEDS ACCORDING TO HIS GLORIOUS RICHES IN CHRIST JESUS.

—PHILIPPIANS 4:19

me! It was the end of my self-sufficiency and the beginning of a total reliance on God. "If I don't have You, I don't have anybody."

You know how the Word says, "He is able to do exceedingly abundantly above all that we could ever ask or think"? In every possible way He provided. The mortgage got paid every month. There were bags of clothing on the porch for all of us. People would leave buckets of fried chicken on the porch twice a week, and we got by!

In spite of everything, there were things I missed about Albert. I needed him because he was a big help with Annie's children, and they were the only ray of sunshine in that total cloud, in the storm of his life. He lived for those little girls. He was an excellent grandfather to them. Every night he picked them up, took them downstairs, and played piano. They either sat and watched TV together, or they played piano together, and he would keep them occupied until I got home and put supper on the table. He was a big help around the house. He always cleaned up the kitchen and the pots.

Albert was not really evil. There are some people who are truly evil. He wasn't evil; he was sick—very sick. I have had to work through a lot of forgiveness with him.

When Albert died, I knew his suffering was over. His mental anguish was over, and he was in a better place. When they finally let me see him at the hospital—and he was obviously dead—I remember standing there, speaking in love, saying, "Albert, I almost have enough faith that if I asked God to bring you back, He would. I wouldn't do that to you because your suffering is over. Your mental anguish and torment are over. You are in a far better place than you have ever been in your life."

Yes, I did learn to love him again because with wisdom and a softer heart, I realized that he was such a sick man. It was not all roses. It was still a love-hate relationship. I loved him; I hated him. I hated him for what he was putting me through during his low points, but I realized I also loved him.

Three weeks before he died, Albert was watching a program about fishing, and he started to sob. He said, "I will never have it. All my life I have wanted a little place in the country with some water, where I could throw in a line and just do some fishing. I am a failure. I will never have it."

I said, "Albert, you are *not* a failure. What does it matter what we have or what we don't have here? You are going to have everything on the other side. God is going to give you a special place in heaven. You won't even have to use a hook; the fish will jump up and sing, 'Praise the Lord, Brother Albert!'" Through his tears he started to laugh.

To the best of my ability, I was trying to love as Christ loves.

Maybe there are some who would think I had lost my mind, and maybe I had. Yes, there was relief when he died, but I *did* love him. I was somehow able to look past what he was doing and see the tortured person he was. I have no idea what it was inside him, what incredible burden he was carrying around, that inclined him to madness. But he was a tormented soul. Unfortunately, it had horrid consequences for me, but I loved him. In the same moment, I also hated him. Life is complex.

I shared many of these things with my pastor's wife years

ago and she said, "Maria, you haven't forgiven him!"

I said, "You're right, I haven't." She prayed with me for forgiveness, and that is how I eventually started working through so many issues and memories and emotions.

I asked myself, "What I am feeling right now? What has triggered this? What is it reminding me of? What old hurt is surfacing?" Even with my last bout of cancer, I have asked God, "What old tendencies are still lodging in me? What unforgiveness lingers? What hidden things are still buried deep inside of me? Help me with my roots of bitterness, Lord. Tell me. Show me. Expose them to me. God, once and for all, I want to be healed. I want to be *totally* healed."

> SEARCH ME, O GOD, AND KNOW MY HEART; TRY ME AND KNOW MY THOUGHTS: AND SEE IF THERE BE ANY WICKED WAY IN ME, AND LEAD ME IN THE WAY EVERLASTING.
>
> —PSALM 139:23–24 (KJV)

In the physical realm, am I healed? Well, I am not coughing my brains out anymore. I don't have sharp pains through my abdomen anymore. So that's a beginning. The rest is in God's hands. I don't understand the Lord or all His ways. Who can? I've given up trying. Who would send His only Son down to earth to die on a cross, to be scourged, beaten, and buffeted so some child molester doesn't have to go to hell? Would I let my child be beaten and crucified for somebody else who deserved hell? I don't understand that kind of love, but I began to love Albert as Christ loved him.

The kind of cancer I have had is called *leiomyosarcoma*, for which there is no chemotherapy or radiation treatment. For my first surgery, they had to remove eighteen inches of my large intestine and eighteen inches of my small intestine. That was in 1988. During 1993, they had to remove a part of my small intestine again and a portion of my liver. Then again in 1997, they had to take out some more of my small intestine, the whole right lobe of my liver, the gall bladder, and another mass of cancer here in my chest cavity in the diaphragm. They had to resection the diaphragm.

In 2001, they had to remove two masses of cancer adjacent to the colon. I also had two masses on my liver, and because I have only one remaining lobe of my liver, I went to Mt. Sinai Hospital to undergo this new innovative method called "radio-frequency ablation." By last year I had lesions again, and two months ago, they took out a large mass of cancer from my abdomen. They did two more radio-frequency ablations on my liver, as there were two masses of cancer on my liver again.

At present the medical records show that I have three lesions in my right lung. So that is the medical status right now. I go through the operations, and there has been a lot of pain, a lot of recuperation, but God has brought me through. This past April, Sloan Kettering Hospital had me listed as terminal. They told me that I am not going to make it. But I have no other choice but to stand on the Word of God that says that by Jesus' stripes I am healed. I have to stand on that, and maybe I am whistling in the dark, but God's Word is all I have to stand on.

My daughter Annie was arguing with me this morning. "What are you going to do? What if your faith doesn't work?"

I said, "Then I will die! What do you want me to tell you, Annie? I wish you had the faith I have."

She said, "I am never going to have what you have. You believe in miracles and I don't!"

Was I upset to find out that things are growing again in my lungs? Yes. You have to be made out of foam rubber not to let it bother you.

A friend called me one night, and she was crying for me: "Oh, Maria, just keep saying, 'God, it is *not* true. God, it is *not* true. God, it is *not* there. God, it is *not* there.'"

I said, "That is *not* a prayer! What kind of a prayer is that? God can't answer that prayer. That is *your* need to be in denial. What if I am heading for Florida, and I get on that plane and say, 'I am *not* going to Florida; I am *not* going to Florida'? When I get off the plane, guess where I'm going to be? You're just saying, 'It is not there. It is not there.' That's not a prayer God can answer.

"Do you want to agree with me in prayer? I am believing in God's Word and agreeing with God's Word that by His stripes I am healed. If you want to pray for me, say, 'In the name of Jesus Christ, I agree with Your Word, that by the stripes He took on His back, Maria is already healed.'"

That is the prayer of agreement that God can honor. I don't need a twenty-line prayer. I need one line, but you may say it twenty times if you want. I am just staying in the Word and believing the Word. I believe with all my heart I am healed. I am waiting for the full manifestation. Would I like Him to go *poof* and it's all gone? I would love it, but if it doesn't work that way, it doesn't work that way. I trust Him.

The fullest manifestation of my healing would be a literal, physical healing. I get upset with people who say, "Oh, you'll have the ultimate healing when you die." Give me a break. That is *not* what we are praying for! We are praying for healing, *not* to die. Of course all my troubles will be over, but I truly believe He will allow me to live through this present cancer. Yes, paradise will be indescribable, but I'm talking about being physically healed of the cancer because I feel to the depth of my being that my life is not over. I am seventy-one years old, but I have so much that I want to give—that which the Lord has for me to do. I have a family who are not all saved. I want to be able to say to the Lord, the way Jesus said to His Father, "Not one whom you have put in my care has been lost to the world." That is what I want to be able to say before my life on earth is through, that they haven't been lost to the world.

REFLECTIONS ON HOLDING THE LORD'S HAND

Maria has learned to give up her self-sufficiency—a hard-won sacrifice. It has not come easily or quickly. She said, "After just over twenty years of being saved, I am finally coming to the point of trusting Him in everything. In my humanness, do I get scared sometimes? Yes, I do. Sometimes I find myself saying to Him, 'Lord, I believe—help Thou my unbelief.' It is very hard. When Peter walked on the water, he took his eyes off Jesus, looked at the waves, and started to sink. I defy anybody who is really going through a storm to tell me he is not going to feel the wind buffeting him, that he is not going to feel the waves beating against his body, and that he is not going to look at the storm! But then Peter came to a point where he started to sink, and he said, 'Lord, save me.' That, I think, is the point at which Jesus wants all of us to get, the point where we realize, 'God, without You, I have nothing.'"

God has sustained Maria every step of the way. In one experience after another God has shown His incredible faithfulness through very dark times. Does she wish she hadn't gone through some of those troubles? Yes. But the one foundational Scripture of her life has been Romans 8:28 (NKJV), which says, "And we *know* [not *hope*, we *know*] that all things work together for good to those who love God, to those who are the called according to His purpose."

Having grown up with such a broken self-image and a low esteem, to find out she was one of *the* called according to God's purpose meant more to Maria than just being called. She knows she is one of those special ones and He cares about her.

Maria told me, "I was fifty-one when I got saved, but for the first time in my life, I have truly been devouring the Bible like the treasure it is. It is like a bank: All this treasure is in the Bible, like having a million-dollar bank account. Yet so many Christians behave like paupers and seem to be thinking, 'I don't want to go to the bank because I don't believe that the money is really there.' I think that when I get there, the bankers are going to say, 'Oh, it's really not in your name; it's in somebody else's.' Or, 'No, you don't deserve it because you didn't do the right thing in order to get the money.'

"Isaiah 53 says God took upon Himself our pains and sorrows and that by the stripes Jesus took on His back, we are healed. Either it is true or it is not true. Either God is a liar or He is telling the truth. There are many verses in Scripture about how Jesus went through crowds and He touched and He healed. Jesus healed them all. Well, He also said, 'I only do what the Father tells me to do.' So then it has got to be true that God really wants us to be healed, and He sent His Word to heal us, Jesus being the living Word."

Today, Maria is appropriating the Word of God. She fluidly paraphrased 2 Corinthians 4:8–11; 16–18: "We are troubled on every side, but we are not distressed; we are perplexed (God, what is going on?), but we are not in despair. We are cast down, but we are not utterly destroyed. We are persecuted, but we are not forsaken. We are always carrying about in our bodies the dying of the Lord Jesus Christ that His resurrection power might be made manifest in our life…. Our outer man may perish (and it does), but our inner man is renewed day by day. For this light affliction, which lasts for a moment, carries for us a far more eternal weight of glory, while we look not at things that are seen but on things that are unseen."

That is what we have to look forward to, but in our talk Maria confessed she feels tired enough to say, "God, I want some of the good stuff now. I'm tired of the pain. I've had my share of being knocked down and popping up again. I must be a boil on the Devil's backside because he comes at me with everything. If he can't get me, he goes after my family. It hurts."

Maria admits she is no candidate for sainthood, in spite of all she has endured. She is bluntly honest about her imperfections.

"I say a lot of unkind things! I have not-so-nice attitudes toward some people. But look at how God viewed David, who did so many wrong things— God saw through to his heart. That is my only saving grace—that God looks through to my heart. The heart is deceitful, but there is also a sweet and good part there. The God-part of my heart supersedes, hopefully, the humanness, the critical nature, and my judgmental attitudes. I am constantly pleading for His mercy and asking Him to overlook my sins. Every night I have to repent for attitudes and words.

I RUN IN THE PATH OF YOUR COMMANDS, FOR YOU HAVE SET MY HEART FREE.

—PSALM 119:32

"Every morning I say, 'Dear Lord, let what I think and say be for Your glory and honor.' Is everything I say and think always to God's glory and honor? No, definitely not. I think nothing of thinking, 'You stupid idiot,' when somebody aggravates me on the telephone. I am thinking it even though I didn't say it, but I am so sad because I am thinking it, and God knows it."

Clearly, God has been able to use the trials in Maria's life to help her reach out to others. Having fought cancer for sixteen years, struggling with loss and emotional pain, she has been able to minister in places where other people can't. She has ministered individually to hundreds of people who have cancer or who have a family member with cancer. How does she do this?

Maria told me, "In the last couple of months—during my most recent recovery period—several sick people have come here. I give them healing prayers. I give them information about how to take care of their health. I give them dietary suggestions. I pray with them. Some get saved. They take the prayer home and the relatives get saved. I am able to say to somebody

THEREFORE WE DO NOT LOSE HEART. THOUGH OUTWARDLY WE ARE WASTING AWAY, YET INWARDLY WE ARE BEING RENEWED DAY BY DAY. FOR OUR LIGHT AND MOMENTARY TROUBLES ARE ACHIEVING FOR US AN ETERNAL GLORY THAT FAR OUTWEIGHS THEM ALL. SO WE FIX OUR EYES NOT ON WHAT IS SEEN, BUT ON WHAT IS UNSEEN. FOR WHAT IS SEEN IS TEMPORARY, BUT WHAT IS UNSEEN IS ETERNAL.

—2 CORINTHIANS 4:16–18

who cries, 'I have shared in much loss. I have been there. I know what you're going through. I have been there.'"

Maria considers it a great privilege to bring God's hope and healing to others through her pain. She is excited to see how it will all work out—in His time. Maria loves being used by the Lord and she loves His handiwork, to be part of His creation and to know that someday she is going to be with Him and be made completely whole. She said, "Yes, I look forward to not having any fat, being slim, healthy, and without a grossly scarred body. If you could see what my poor body looks like. I have had thirteen cancer surgeries in sixteen years; that's a lot of stitches. I have been opened up many times. I know that eventually I'm going to be perfect and I'm going to be with Jesus forever. 'Surely, surely, goodness and mercy shall follow me all the days of my life, and I will dwell in the house of the Lord forever.' I look not on things that are seen, but on things that are unseen. That gives me strength. That gives me the courage to walk through the storms. There is no other way. I'll hold His hand."

My interview with Maria was filled with a plethora of emotions. I sat speechless for a while. I certainly took a roller coaster ride on that old couch. She offered dessert, but for once, I had no appetite. Too many thoughts, images, and words were criss-crossing through my mind. We soon hugged good-bye in the same spot we hugged hello. As I lifted my heavy briefcase into the rental car, Maria stepped toward me with a trusting half-smile and lifted her knit shirt high enough for me to get a full view of her stomach. It bore no resemblance to a human stomach. I'd say it looked more like a topographical map. Tracks, lines, dips, twists—high and low terrain—smooth patches and then suddenly rough ones. Kind of like Maria's life.

More than any other factor,
the condition of your attitude
will determine the quality of
your relationships with other
people; whether you can turn a
problem into a blessing, whether
you become a victim of defeat or
a student of success.

—John Maxwell

CHAPTER FOUR

Doris: Forgiving Those Who Are Closest

*S*ometimes it's not an incident or a season of pain that we face. Sometimes it's a lifetime of hurts and disappointments. As women, many of us rely on the tenderness and encouragement that comes through relationships with our mothers, sisters, daughters, and granddaughters. But what if those are the very people who bring us the most pain? And what is it like when each of those people has hurt us deeply?

I drove to the Baltimore area from my home in northern Virginia on a sunny Tuesday afternoon to meet Doris. She is a full-figured, flaming redhead who is also full of a zest for life. Proud of her roots, Doris wore a tiny Irish flag pinned alongside her American one.

"Were you born with all that red hair?" I asked quite curiously.

"Yes, of course, but let's just say it's turned lots of colors along the way." She winked as her Irish eyes smiled.

Doris did not want to meet at her home, so we spent the lovely afternoon parked at a corner table in a cafe on the Inner Harbor. I soon learned that Doris's life is laced with deep wounds she received from those closest to her. She has experienced a great deal of pain and loss in family relation-ships, and she began by sharing the most distant memories of her childhood.

IN HER OWN WORDS: DORIS'S STORY

I got so many beatings from my mother and father. It was serious physical abuse, not just spankings. We lived in Philly when I was a kid, and then we moved to Baltimore. We had a decent living standard. My father worked—he was a bookie actually. If he was doing well and his numbers were good, everything was fine and it was feast time. But if he didn't do well that day, watch out! He was volcanic. The neighborhood where I lived had a lot of violence—my friends didn't get hit the way we got hit, but we never really talked about the abuse with anybody. Everything was always done for appearances.

My father would rub his finger on the side of his nose, which was a signal that a beating was coming. I had one brother and one sister. My brother, Joe, was a year older and my sister, Margaret, was two years younger. Margaret and I would ask our dad, "What are we doing wrong? What are we doing wrong?" If there were people out and around, he would never let anybody know that a beating was imminent, but then when nobody was there—he could be smiling and waving good-bye to company and then turn around and grab us by the throats and start beating us. It was sometimes a ver-bal volley:

"Come over here."

"No, because I know you are going to hit me."

"I promise I am not going to hit you."

"No, I know you are going to hit me."

"No, I promise you!"

"No, you always say that, Daddy, but you always do."

"Not this time—I absolutely promise ..."

Of course, as soon as I got within arm's reach, he would grab me. It was a kind of terrorism. We lived in railroad rooms [in which the narrow rooms in the unit are all arranged in a straight line], so Margaret and I would run to the end of the rooms until there was no place else to go. Then we would jump out the window and just cower in terror, knowing he was coming for us.

My brother Joe was never hit in his life, but Margaret and I were both beaten like dogs—both of us. I am talking about lying on the floor and being kicked in the stomach until we vomited, being punched and kicked to the point of not being able to go to school for days and days. My mother would call up and say, "They have bad colds."

My mother often said, "I wish I could send you two back. I would have taken three boys instead of you two girls!" The sun rose and set on my brother Joe.

I used to look at other people, even when I was a kid, and think, "I wonder how come their parents love them, and I wonder why ours don't love us." I remember saying to my sister, "Margaret, you know what? Maybe if we pray to die, Mommy will be happy."

Margaret would respond, "I don't want to die! You can pray for *you* to die. I don't want to die!"

I said, "Okay, I will pray for *me* to die." I was five or six years old.

Mother's constant message was, "If only I didn't have you, I would be happy." And that was repeated again and again and again.

The beatings were less frequent during our teen years, but the verbal and emotional abuse never ceased. We would travel from Baltimore to the shore a couple times a year. In the summer of 1949, we three teenagers were swimming out to a diving dock. I got there first and climbed up on the dock.

I watched Joe swim toward me. He broke his stride, screamed for help, went down, and never came up again. He died of a heart attack. He was only eighteen years old.

The day of his funeral, I remember everybody had left the house, and Margaret and I were sitting down on the front stoop when my mother looked at me said, "You, you useless thing. God left *you*, you useless thing, and took the only person I ever loved. I will never forgive you for living. I will *never* forgive you for living."

I had so many beatings in my life, so many things said to me, but I think that was the first time my *soul* was wounded, hearing my mother say that. I was *deeply* scarred.

I WILL GIVE YOU THE TREASURES OF DARKNESS, RICHES STORED IN SECRET PLACES, SO THAT YOU MAY KNOW THAT I AM THE LORD, THE GOD OF ISRAEL, WHO SUMMONS YOU BY NAME.

—ISAIAH 45:3

As years passed, I tried to get into a relationship with God. I went to my first prayer meeting and walked right out because I heard all these women say, "O, Daddy God! Father God, dear Abba! I love you and I trust you."

I thought, *Father God? In a pig's eye would I trust You! I know what Father God is like; I know what Daddy is like. I'm going to trust You? As soon as I get within Your reach, You're going to pulverize me.*

It was a very difficult phase from then until the day when I gloriously found out that God really *did* love me and that I *could* call Him my Father. Now I know He's the Father I could run to and that He's always there for me. It's a whole different life; it's a whole different walk. And you know when Scripture says, "He restores my soul," it is incremental. The Bible talks about line upon line, precept upon precept, here a little, there a little ... the knowledge of God comes (Isa. 28:9–11 KJV). And it's true. But it's always "a little." Many times we don't see it, but in retrospect we can look back and say, "He was there all along." At the time, I couldn't imagine He was there all along. I couldn't imagine He was there at all.

After our first daughter, Amy, was born, it was evident she had physical problems—multiple handicaps. She was injured at birth from the use of forceps. Then she started having seizures at about two months of age. Testing showed she also had cystic fibrosis. It got to the point where she was having about ten seizures a day—every day. No amount of medication would hold her for more than a week, and then the seizures would start again. I was about twenty-nine years old. It was a very painful and difficult time, and all during those years, the marital stress grew more and more unbearable. Our trouble made us drift apart, not draw closer. My husband shut down and became angry.

Amy died before her fourth birthday. Michelle was only three, and she said to me the next morning, "Mommy, you know what? Amy came to see me last night, and she told me to tell you that she has no more pain, and she is very happy where she is." *Wow.* Although I was not yet a Christian, I wondered about heaven, and I really believed her because I hadn't yet told her or her little sister that Amy died. They had no way of knowing.

I replied, "You know, honey, when Amy was here she

never spoke. She could only say 'mama' and 'no.' How did she tell you she was happy?"

> CAN A MOTHER FORGET THE BABY AT HER BREAST AND HAVE NO COMPASSION ON THE CHILD SHE HAS BORNE? THOUGH SHE MAY FORGET, I WILL NOT FORGET YOU! SEE, I HAVE ENGRAVED YOU ON THE PALMS OF MY HANDS; YOUR WALLS ARE EVER BEFORE ME.
>
> —ISAIAH 49:15–16

Michelle said, "Mommy, that's funny! She thought it in her head, and I knew what she was saying." That was about as close to the truth as we could get. She "thought" it in her head! I absolutely knew that my little Amy was telling me, "I am in a better place."

My little ones helped me get back to normal. I was very grateful to have them to come home to after Amy's funeral. There was a tremendous sense of relief when Amy died because there was such incredible suffering. Several weeks before her death she had a seizure that left her totally paralyzed. There was no life for my sweet little girl.

Did I grieve? Of course, I grieved! I remember looking at her in the casket. I said, "It's over, little Amy. Nothing is going to hurt you again. Nobody is ever going cut you, prod you, bind you, or do anything to you. You will never be hurt again. You are *totally* free! Your anguish and torment are over. You are in a far better place than you have ever been in your life."

After Amy died, my husband turned inward and we became "married singles." Occasionally, his anger spilled into the household. I was able to absorb the verbal abuse, but Michelle was the one who really suffered because her father didn't like her. He was never verbally abusive with our youngest one, Julie, but he was constantly harping on Michelle. He let his feelings be known that he did not like her. Julie became his favorite. The sun that had shone on Amy was transferred over to Julie.

Michelle and Julie both grew angry in their teen years and they both married angry, violent men. They both divorced and had various troubled relationships.

And they both got heavily involved with drugs. Julie left home when she was eighteen and had a baby at twenty-one. This was about the time I totally surrendered my life to God. Clearly, I had so many areas that needed God's healing. After Julie's baby, Jennifer, was born, she would call up and say, "Listen, I can't take this kid anymore. I need a break from her, so come and get her." We would get in the car and drive—any time, day or night—and sometimes we would go into her apartment, and the baby was there but not Julie. She would give us an address, and we would go there—it would be an empty apartment. Julie would just leave her with anybody.

My husband and I never talked about it. We were just there for the baby. I think baby Jennifer brought back memories of our sweet Amy. My husband softened and was a good grandpa. When Jennifer turned two, Julie left her at our door and never came back. My husband died of a heart attack a year later. I couldn't contact Julie about her father's death because we didn't know where she was. We put the word out on the street near where we heard she was living, but she never tried to reach us.

When Michelle was twenty-one and out of the house, she was involved with drugs, being promiscuous, and heading toward destruction. She was functioning—working at an incredibly good job in commodity trading—but she struggled with drug addiction. She was in a drug program as a teenager, graduated high school in a drug program, and struggled with cocaine until she was thirty-five years old. She just turned forty. She's been clean for the past five years.

I remember perfectly the day I got the call about Julie, who was dying in the hospital. A nurse called from a hospital two hours away and said, "Julie has been in the hospital for several days, and she has slipped into a coma. She had given us your name, and we think you ought to come."

I arranged for [then] seven-year-old Jennifer to go home from school with a friend, called Michelle, picked her up from work, and we drove there. When we got to the desk, we were told we had to put on masks and gowns before we could go into the room. She was in an HIV ward. In 1992, there were still many misconceptions about AIDS. People were afraid to breathe near AIDS patients, let alone touch them.

The station head nurse was curt with Michelle and me. I asked, "Is something wrong?"

"Yes, I would say something is wrong."

I said, "I am not understanding. I got a phone call that my daughter was dying, and I came as soon as possible. I am getting an attitude from you that I don't understand."

She said, "You want to know what the attitude is all about? Your daughter came out of her coma last night, pulled all the tubes out of herself, and we found her in her wheelchair down in the parking lot shooting drugs!"

By the time I saw her in the hospital, Julie was in her upper twenties and weighed less than sixty pounds. Michelle and I got to her door and we were putting on our masks and gowns outside of her room. We could hear her on the phone in there, saying to somebody, "I don't know where I'm going to get the money, but I *will* get the money. I will get the money somehow. Don't worry about it. Just *promise* me you're going to bring the stuff."

Michelle dug her fingers into my arm. "Mom, she's in there arranging for a fix. I'm going to go in there and punch her lights out!"

"Michelle, I haven't seen her in five years. If we went to the zoo to see a zebra, would you get angry at the zebra for having stripes? If we went to see a leopard, would you get mad at the leopard for having spots? She is a drug addict. That is what she is. That is what she does. If you're going to go in to punch out her lights, please don't come in. I haven't seen her for five years. And this is my baby. Don't go in if you're going in with anger."

Michelle calmed down. We walked into the room; I looked into the bed and saw a skeleton. Julie had big blue eyes and long eyelashes that you could trip over, but I looked into this bed and thought, *Who is this skeleton lying in this bed?*

Julie looked up and said into the phone, "Oh, my God; it's my mother." She didn't know they had called me. She said, "It's my mother and my sister. I'll call you back later."

I walked over, took off my mask, and gathered her into my arms. I kissed her all over her face because she was still my baby.

Saying Good-bye to Julie

I don't understand drug addiction. I don't know what that pull is like. I only know that it was important that I saw Julie and that we got to talk. We talked about the loss of her leg, which had been amputated for medical reasons. We talked about her daughter. We talked about different things.

Some time later, we were called back to the hospital. It was finally time to say good-bye to her as she had gone into total kidney failure and fallen back into a coma.

I held her limp hand and said, "Julie, I know that you can't speak on the outside, but you can hear me on the inside. And now it is time to rededicate your life to the Lord. I will give you that prayer one line at a time. I will give you time to repeat it inside yourself."

So I said one line at a time to her. At the end of the prayer, when I said, "I receive You now and rededicate my life to You now as my Savior and my Lord," tears were streaming down both sides of her face. I said, "Michelle! She's crying. She can hear everything we're saying to her!"

Michelle, who was dabbling in drugs and who had still not given her life back to God, was holding her other hand, and said, "Oh, Julie, how I wish there was some way that you could let us know! Will you please let us know you can hear us?" With two fingers, Julie pressed the middle of her sister's hand. God gave her that grace. We went crazy—hooting and hollering and praising.

Julie was connected to so many tubes and was suffering, so after many discussions with the doctors and much prayerful consideration, I decided to discontinue her life support. I said, "I am going to tell you the same thing I told your sister, Amy, before she died: Go on and leave this body behind because it is no longer serving you. I have asked Jesus to send angels of light to guide you over that River Jordan. Cross over, Julie, because you will be whole, and you will be healed, and you will know peace—something you haven't known in years.

"You will see Daddy." (She didn't even know her father had died.) "You will see Amy and Little Grandma" (my sweet grandmother). I mentioned more people, and then I said, "And then when it's my turn, my dearest Julie, I will see you again, and what a day that will be! No more tears, no more separation, no more heartaches. We'll be together forever."

I kissed her once more, and the life support was turned off. The doctors unhooked the machine. Her chest just gave a little flutter, and she left this world. I said, "If God wants you to live, you will live, and if He wants to take you home, He is going to take you home." He took her home.

Twenty-seven years earlier, I said those very same words to Amy when she was dying. The difference was that the second time, I was absolutely committed to Jesus, familiar with His wonderful promises, and completely confident in the "far better place" that my girls were going to.

When I gathered her things from the night table drawer in the hospital, I found a Bible with maybe forty sticky notes in it and writing all over the margins. She somehow never really lost her contact with God. She had her Bible there. It wasn't a brand-new Bible; it was all curled and worn with notes all over the place.

AFTER THE EARTHQUAKE CAME A FIRE, BUT THE LORD WAS NOT IN THE FIRE. AND AFTER THE FIRE CAME A GENTLE WHISPER.

—1 KINGS 19:12

There was such deep grieving and sorrow; drug addict or no drug addict, she was my baby. It was a very painful thing for me. I could still cry about Julie because she was such a beautiful girl, very bright, very artistic. She could do anything. She could play the piano. She'd had six years of dance lessons, and she could fly across the room. She was the quintessence of grace. She did everything beautifully, but she could never beat that addiction. She refused to surrender to God until the very end. Yes, there was anger inside me that somebody could do that to her life, but I don't understand that level of addiction. I am grateful to God that He gave me the last four days of her life in which to really make our reconciliation.

It is incredible to say this, but God can use even the worst circumstances for His glory. I had prayed with a young Jewish man about six o'clock that morning, and he offered his heart, mind, and soul to Messiah. Julie died about four o'clock in the afternoon. As we were leaving the hospital, the young man called out to me, "Doris, I heard. I'm so sorry. Listen, Doris, I may never ever see you again in this life, but I *will* see you up in heaven. I will remind you of this day. I never knew your daughter, Julie, but when I get to heaven, I am going to say to her, 'You know when you were in the hospital dying, I was in the hospital too, and your mom prayed with me, and the day you died, I got eternal life!'"

You see, that is the victory! The promise we have in Christ Jesus wasn't just His life and His death, it was His life and His death and His resurrection! Because He lives, we will live. That is quite a victory! "Oh, death, where is thy sting, O grave ..."

Forgiving a Deep Hurt

The words I spoke at Amy's bedside and the words I spoke at my husband's bedside and the words I spoke at Julie's bedside would be the very words I would speak at the deathbeds of my mother and my sister in the months that followed.

When I knew Julie was dying, I went home that night

and called my mother, who always believed Julie had stolen her expensive bracelet. I'm sure she did not, but the story is too long. My mother remained very vindictive and bitter. She said, "I will never forgive her!" She had her legal will changed, removing Julie from it.

"Mom, I need to talk to you about Julie."

She said, "Don't talk to me about that little S.O.B. I don't *ever* want her name mentioned to me again."

"Well, I'm going to have to mention it to you, Mom, because I saw her today, and she is very sick."

She said, "I don't care. Good, I'm glad she's sick! I wish every horrible thing that could happen to anybody will happen to her. That's what she deserves."

"Well, Mom, she lost her leg. Is that enough for you?"

She snapped, "*No*, that wouldn't be enough. She *deserved* to lose her leg!" (Ironically, two weeks before my mother died, she had her left leg amputated.)

I said, "Listen, Mom, I don't care whether you want to hear me or not, I have to get this off my chest. I don't believe Julie stole your jewelry, although you do. You've said you'll never forgive her. Well, the girl is dying, and I don't want her to die with your unforgiveness on her soul, so I am going to ask you to please forgive her."

"Oh, don't give me that. That pathological liar—I wouldn't believe her."

"Mom! The girl weighs less than sixty pounds. She's dying."

My mother's voice caught. "Is she really dying?"

"Yes, she is really dying. Will you do it for me, Mom? Would you please forgive her, because you may die before she does, and I don't want you to die with the unforgiveness on your soul."

She said hesitantly, "Yes, I'll forgive her. What do you want me to say?"

"I want you to say, 'Julie, I forgive you for stealing my

jewelry.' Even though I don't think she did, but you do. I want you to say you forgive her."

She said, "Okay," and repeated to me, "Julie, I forgive you for stealing my jewelry."

Then I said, "As long as we're talking about forgiveness, there's something else that's been on my heart for years. Two times in my life you told me you wouldn't forgive me for something. One was on the day I was born. You later said that I rejected your breast, and you would never forgive me for that. I want you to forgive me for rejecting your breast the day I was born."

"Doris, this is ridiculous—"

"No, it's important, Mom, because I don't want your unforgiveness on my soul, and I don't want you to have it toward me."

So she said, "Okay, I forgive you." I knew at that point the Holy Spirit was at work because all of a sudden she quieted down. The anger was not there.

I said, "Now, we have to go one step further. The day Joe was buried you looked at me and said, 'You useless thing. God took the only person I ever loved and left *you*—you useless thing! I will never forgive you for that.' Mom, I want you to forgive me for living the day Joe died."

"Doris, I am *not* talking about this."

I said, "No! It's been over forty years, and we have never *once* addressed it. I want you to forgive me for living the day Joe died."

So she did.

I said, "Let's go one step further. You said, 'God took the only person I ever loved,' and that's true. You've blocked everybody else out, Mom, including God. I want you to forgive God for taking your son from you."

She did that, and then I led her through the sinner's prayer. She gave her heart to Jesus. My mother mellowed considerably in her final months, and we shared some meaningful and healing moments.

Again, that is God using the deepest pits of our circumstances for His glory. Deep in my heart, even after all the physical and emotional torture, I didn't want my mother to die and go to hell. My father also got saved in his eleventh hour. I was able to pray with him before he died. My sister and my brother-in-law have also come to know Him. That is part of why God has me here. Little by little He restores our souls, our minds, our wills, and our emotions. It is incremental sometimes, line upon line, precept upon precept, here a little, there a little. That's hope.

PRAISE BE TO THE GOD AND FATHER OF OUR LORD JESUS CHRIST, THE FATHER OF COMPASSION AND THE GOD OF ALL COMFORT, WHO COMFORTS US IN ALL OUR TROUBLES, SO THAT WE CAN COMFORT THOSE IN ANY TROUBLE WITH THE COMFORT WE OURSELVES HAVE RECEIVED FROM GOD. FOR JUST AS THE SUFFERINGS OF CHRIST FLOW OVER INTO OUR LIVES, SO ALSO THROUGH CHRIST OUR COMFORT OVERFLOWS.

—2 CORINTHIANS 1:3–5

My granddaughter Jennifer really thought for a long time that her mother was coming back to her. It was very traumatic. Two or three years ago, Jennifer started pulling away from me, and this past year, she has really expressed anger and rage. She never had closure because she never got to see her mother before the death. She was only seven years old, and it would have been far too traumatic for her to have seen Julie in that condition.

Jen has a father out there somewhere. I pray for that man every single day that he will get saved. Last week, Jen was here with a friend and I heard her say, "I have had to forgive my mother for everything, because if my mother hadn't left me at this house, I would be dead by now. I wouldn't be alive if it wasn't for my grandmother. I have had to work through a lot of forgiveness for my mother and my father." So I praise God that she is coming along. It's been yet another hard journey.

Jennifer was brought up on the Word of God. She has been backslidden for the last couple of years, but she's coming back because she knows better. She sat here last week and said, "I've tried running. God is the only answer. There is no other answer."

She needs somebody. I pray Romans 4:17 every day: "God ... calls things that are not as though they were." I do the same thing, thanking Him ahead of time for sending her a good nurturing Christian mate who will love her and cherish her for the rest of her life. "Give her somebody other than me to care for her," I ask God.

To anybody with a rebellious teen I'd say, "Just try and love them the way God loves you—unconditionally. That certainly doesn't mean no discipline, no rules, but at this juncture, she's nineteen years old, so my parenting days are over. Now I can only guide and advise. She's an adult, and she's going to have to make her own decisions and face her own consequences. All I can do is keep praying for her and keep on loving her."

I had to pray, "Create in me a clean heart, O Lord. Renew a right spirit in me," because my spirit was wrong. I was angry at Jennifer. I was disappointed in her. I wanted her to change, but you know what? I am not in control. I had to say, "God, I take my hands off her. You are her Father. I can't take care of her; You're going to have to take care of her." When she was living away from home, weeks would go by when I wouldn't hear from her. Was I concerned? You better believe I was concerned, but there was nothing I could do about it—except to pray.

When she came home, she said many hurtful things. She has been through so much.

I said to her, "Jennifer, I hear what you're telling me, and all I'm going to tell you is that I love you more. I love you more than whatever you are doing or saying to me."

She just looked at me like *Are you nuts?* But you know something? That's what she needs to hear because if I return hate for hate, then God cannot work between us.

Isaiah 55:9 tells us, "As the heavens are higher than the earth, so are my ways higher than your ways and my thoughts than your thoughts."

This is why, to me, speaking the Word is not "name it and claim it." It is speaking God's Word, because He says that "just as the rain and snow come down from heaven and water the earth, they don't return back to it, but they give seed to the sower and bread to the reaper, so does My Word go forth from My mouth and accomplishes that which pleases Me and prospers where it is sent." (See Isaiah 55:10–11.) You can't fight stuff like that! You see, the truth of that meets me at the level of my deepest need. *That's* encouragement!

I have a vision for Jen. She is going to be preaching the

Word of God someday. She is going to be used so mightily. This girl knows the Bible inside out. I know the child that she was. I know what's been invested in her. God is going to use her for His glory. I know that to the depths of my being. I've said to her, "You could run through every alley of your mind to try to satisfy your soul. You are never going to outrun Him. And you could run through every alley of this earth to try to satisfy yourself, and you are never going to find any peace until you come back to Him."

She responded, "Yeah, yeah, Grandma."

I think in her mind, coming home was an act of sacrifice. She came home to be stuck with the old lady again. And there is a gradual breaking of the hard ground. She has openly told me every day that she loves me—every day! When her friend was in trouble, she brought her here and said, "Grandma, talk to her about God." That says a lot.

I prayed with her very pierced and tattooed friend, and Jen looked up and said, "I tried running; there is no place to run."

Yes, getting past self-pity is a discipline. We make decisions. One little thing I know—when we do wrong things, we get wrong results. What you sow is what you are going to reap. To me, self-pity is one of the most harmful emotions anybody can have. It doesn't mean we're always going to be happy about what's going on in our lives, but people who wallow in their self-pity are only headed to a deeper ditch.

You ask me about the rejection? That has been a stronghold over my life. But you know, bottom line: I am no different from you, because if you knew that somebody had really very little respect for you or thought very little of you, even though they are not really a part of your life, it would hurt you. It would hurt you because we all need to be loved. If nothing else, I have come to the point of knowing I am loved.

I wish I had been taken care of more lovingly by the people in my family. If I wanted to depict the greatest sadness right now, it is for all the wasted and lost time with my family. The most frustrating thing in my life has been not being able to share the things of God with my family— Michelle in particular, because she is my only living child and she still rejects God. I always say, "You could come laughing

AND SO WE KNOW AND RELY ON THE LOVE GOD HAS FOR US. GOD IS LOVE. WHOEVER LIVES IN LOVE LIVES IN GOD, AND GOD IN HIM.

—1 JOHN 4:16

or you could come crying, but come you will." Michelle is still holding on and doing things her way. She still is choosing to come crying. All she has to do is let go and go with the flow, but she refuses to do that. So she holds on to the brambles and gets scraped on the rocks along the edge of the river. She is getting scratched and buffeted on the rocks, but sooner or later she is going to have to let go and let God take her where He wishes. He will take anyone in His love and really heal them the way they need to be healed.

Before I was a believer, I used to obsess about the hurts my parents caused me. "Just wait until you're old; I'll get you back." I was determined that someday I was going to get revenge.

After salvation, I had to give that up. It was an act of my own will that I had to give that up. I had a little assignment book that somebody had given me, and I used to mark down whenever my mother would hit me. I would count the blows—one, two, three, four, and so on—and make marks in the book. My mother found it and asked, "What are all those marks in that book?"

I said, "Those were all the times you hit me. I'm counting them, and when I get big you are getting them all back."

Years and years later, when I was in my forties, I was on a silent retreat and the priest said, "I want you to envision Jesus standing in front of you and taking you in His arms." I suddenly saw myself as though I were watching a TV set. I saw myself as a little tiny girl, and I walked over to Jesus and sat on His lap. Why I was a little girl and not the adult that I was, I don't know. But that was that wounded little girl. I still get sad for her sometimes.

I saw myself sit on Jesus' lap because that is what He told me to do, and I suddenly wriggled off His lap and walked out of the picture. I thought, *Where did I go?* I just walked out of the picture, and all of a sudden I walked back over to Jesus and I handed Him the book with all the marks. I left it with Him.

I know that was a turning point in my life. That was the beginning of the restoration of my soul. I gave Him the "hit book."

That's how I've worked through all these things. I think of my father, and I realize if he knew the harm he was causing us, he never would have done it. There was a good side to him; I do have some nice memories. He loved plants and gardens. I also love plants, and I have a green thumb I got from him. He wasn't an evil man, but he grew up in violence. The grace of

God has enabled me to look past a person's hurtful words and deeds and see the hurting person behind it. So I have just tried, to the best of my ability, not to hurt people back.

I tried to be super mom to my kids. I was determined I was going to be the best mother I could possibly be because never once in my life did my mother hold me close or tell me she loved me. When I had my own children, I made sure that every single day of their lives I said, "Thank you for being mine. Of all the mommies in the world you could have chosen to belong to, thank you for being mine; I love you so much." I went to the extreme of not disciplining them the way I should have. The loss of Amy caused them to get away with a lot. My husband was strict and he would (fittingly) punish them. As soon as his back was turned, I would take the punishment away. I wanted them to love me; I didn't want them not to like me. I wanted to be their friend. It didn't exactly work out that way, did it?

After Julie died, my mother was visiting, and I remember saying to her, "I have one great consolation. I believe I was the best mother I could have been to the girls. I did and gave all that I could."

My mother grew very quiet, then timidly asked, "Was I a good mother, Doris?"

I said, "Well, you always made sure we had food in our stomachs and clothes on our backs." I could have said so much more, but God desires that we do not return hurt for hurt.

REFLECTING ON THE JOY OF FORGIVENESS

We could all learn a lot about joy from Doris. She has a big smile and exudes excitement and energy when she walks into a room. How is this possible, given all she has endured and experienced?

Doris admits she doesn't understand it all, but says it is

truly from God because His Word promises each of us, "The joy of the Lord is my strength" (Neh. 8:10). He has given Doris the ability to look beneath the wrapping to find the blessing. Does it mean she doesn't cry? She claims she should have ruts down her face for all of the times she has cried.

But she has enough of Christ within her that she walks around knowing she is an overcomer by His grace. Doris is more than a conqueror. Like her, we each must remind ourselves that nothing can separate us from the love of God that is in Christ Jesus.

He tells us in His Word, "Who shall separate us from the love of Christ? Shall trouble or hardship or persecution or famine or nakedness or danger or sword? ... No, in all these things we are more than conquerors through him who loved us. For I am convinced that neither death nor life, neither angels nor demons, neither the present nor the future, nor any powers, neither height nor depth, nor anything else in all creation, will be able to separate us from the love of God that is in Christ Jesus" (Rom. 8:35, 37–39). We have to stand on that, to walk in that.

God has allowed Doris the incredible privilege of ministering to many others one to

GIVE, AND IT WILL BE GIVEN TO YOU. A GOOD MEASURE, PRESSED DOWN, SHAKEN TOGETHER AND RUNNING OVER, WILL BE POURED INTO YOUR LAP. FOR WITH THE MEASURE YOU USE, IT WILL BE MEASURED TO YOU.

—LUKE 6:38

one. Through the trials she has faced in her life, Doris has been led to triumph. When other people see her, they are amazed that she has such deep, abiding joy. They are curious about it, and it gives Doris a chance to explain the reason for the hope within her. She said, "I love that because, to me, the most important thing is pointing people toward Jesus. If I have one main thrust in my life, it is that people would come to a saving knowledge of Jesus Christ. I get such joy from sharing Him."

As we ended our time of talking and laughing together, the tears began to flow freely. As she wept softly, Doris spoke these words: "It has taken over twenty years, but I have finally come to the point of knowing I am His beloved child! I really am. I don't even know why I'm crying. Maybe it's just because I've had a lifetime of not being able to really fully comprehend that I'm loved. With each day and with each thing that goes on in my life, I understand His love a little more. I feel His love a little more. When I am alone, I am praising Him with my whole heart. I look at every flower in my garden every morning. I say to the morning glories, 'Aren't you wonderful, glorifying God just as you were meant to do, doing just what God created you to do.' Knowing that I'm part of His creation, I look up at the sky and say, 'God, You do such beautiful work! You do such wonderful work! You are just amazing.'"

Doris never read from a Bible or a devotional or a reference book when she shared all the Bible verses during our interview. I was quite taken by her incredible love and broad knowledge of the Word. Though life has given her many battle scars, all I could see were beauty marks of a woman who truly understands forgiveness and grace.

We all know people who have been made much meaner and more irritable and more intolerable to live with by suffering; it is not right to say that all suffering perfects. It only perfects one type of person ... the one who accepts the call of God in Christ Jesus.

—*Oswald Chambers*

CHAPTER FIVE

Serena:
Receiving God's Care
in the Confusion

*S*erena greeted me in her quaint two-story townhouse on the outskirts of Chicago. Thought she is nearing sixty, her beautiful African-American skin and her broad smile suggest she is two decades younger. I've been known to complain to my sisters of color that "black skin lies!"

Serena's name matches her persona; she is demure, with a hint of shyness. I was put in touch with her by my pastor's wife, who happens to be her cousin.

I had the great privilege of speaking at one of Willow Creek's national conferences on a Friday. I then braved some serious Chicago traffic to interview Serena that evening. Her daughters were out for the evening, and she lit several aromatic candles to create a soothing atmosphere. She was tired from a long week at the office, and I was tired from wearing heels and talking all day at the conference. I was so glad Serena would be doing most of the talking. We both enjoyed kicking our shoes off and curling up at the ends of two overstuffed couches.

SERENA'S STORY: IN HER OWN WORDS

I am a city girl, born in Brooklyn in 1944, a middle child from an average- to lower-income household. I was raised in a Catholic school: Saint Ambrosia—a lot of Irish folks!

When I was a kid, I was a people pleaser. I always felt that no one was going to love me just for me. So I would do whatever anyone wanted before they even asked for it. I was always very easygoing. If anyone needed something I was there; they used to call me "No Sweat Serena." I would never tell if I was hurt by something that someone did because they might turn around and blame me for my mistakes. So I would never, ever speak about any feelings.

I started working during high school when I was sixteen. That was what was expected of us. We didn't have aspirations of going to college. I always wanted to be a secretary—that was fine for me.

I was a nominal Catholic. I went to church while I was in school because I had to, but when I got old enough, my mother couldn't make me go. Still, whenever I was bad, that is where I went. I just always believed that I never could measure up to what God expected of me. No one would ever think I didn't have self-esteem, because I looked confident on the outside.

From the age of eighteen, I was working and spending every dime I made. I lived at home until I was almost twenty-nine, and then I got

I HAVE LOVED YOU WITH AN EVERLASTING LOVE; I HAVE DRAWN YOU WITH LOVING-KINDNESS.

—JEREMIAH 31:3

an apartment with my friend. During that time I went with some friends on a weekend called DeColores, a movement within the Catholic Church. On that weekend I felt genuinely loved for the first time—and by Jesus! I never would have even dreamed it. I don't know when it happened and I don't know how, but I knew that Jesus loved me. I didn't really even know Jesus before that.

I struggled with low self-esteem then, and I sometimes still struggle with it today, that feeling of unworthiness. That was a tremendous thing within my marriage too; I didn't know how to deal with feelings. I would usually just push them away, dig a hole, and put them in there because I never dealt with conflict in my single life. I shielded myself.

When I met my husband, I could tell he was not really my type, but he seemed like a nice guy. I got very tired of meeting guys who were just looking to get you into bed. Bill was three years older than me, and though he wasn't a good dresser, he was decent looking. And there was a part of him that seemed genuinely interested in me. So I started dating him, and we went out for a year and a half before we got married.

I didn't know much about his temper; it didn't show until later on. He did tell me that he had a couple of nervous breakdowns and that he was manic-depressive. To me, that wasn't so bad! Really—looking back, I think I was a little naïve—stupid is more accurate. The real trouble started when we decided to get married.

Before the marriage, I didn't pick up on the problem. During our engagement there was a time I felt I shouldn't go through with the wedding, but I thought if I broke up with him there wouldn't be anybody else for me. I just didn't know how to deal with it. I was screaming inside, and I wanted to tell somebody that I knew there was trouble, but it was too scary.

I even met his psychiatrist because Bill wanted me to. Looking back at that time, aside from his anger outbursts, Bill was a pretty decent guy. I knew nothing about manic depression. I didn't see him depressed or anything bad; he was just a very angry guy. But that anger kept building more and more.

The abuse did start before our marriage. It was one or two in the morning, and we were talking. He said something, and I responded with something like, "Oh, no, forget that. That's crazy. Are you for real?" He was sitting next to me and smacked my arm! I am talking about "slam!" Though I was flabbergasted, I didn't say anything. I just sat there for what seemed like an eternity.

He didn't apologize. He just said, "Just don't get nasty with your mouth like that!" I acted like it never happened. But I remember screaming again to myself, *What did I do? What have I done? What do I do?*

That's when I think maybe fear crept in. I wouldn't have been fearful in breaking up with him at that time. It wasn't fear that kept me with him, like a fear that he would come after me. It was too soon; it hadn't developed into that. I just didn't know how to deal with anything like that. There was a part of me that felt I did love him. I was in love with the idea of marriage, a lifelong dream, a symbol.

Later, when we were first married, I came home one night and he had prepared dinner and bought roses to say "I love you." I felt so loved. Times when he would meet me at the train station, I would be so excited to get off the train because I knew he would be there.

But quickly our marriage went bad. For instance, once Bill was sitting at the kitchen table and I was by the sink at the other end of the counter, and for whatever reason he threw a whole container of milk at me, drenching me and the floor. He said, "Clean it up." I cleaned it up. I don't know when it was, whether it was that night or later on, he said, "I am so sorry. I see you dripping with milk, and I am ordering you to clean it up!" So he would apologize and the cycle would begin again.

It was much different in the later years than in the earlier years of our marriage. There was a definite deterioration. Yes, the people who knew him then thought he was a great guy because they had no idea about his manic depression. He was hospitalized a couple of times, and we moved a lot.

If I ever asked for anything, he got angry. But Bill would turn around and, on his own, take me to the store and say, "I'm going to buy you that piece of jewelry, the one you said you liked," even though it was over what we thought we could do in a budget. It was a matter of control, absolutely. He had to control everything.

He started having psychotic episodes and nervous breakdowns. He obviously had stopped taking his medication and was acting bizarre one night when he came home and told me, "You just lied." He slapped my face and took me near the picture of Jesus and said, "Now apologize."

He would be hospitalized and undergo shock treatments, then go back to work, saying, "I need to prove to myself I can pick myself back up again." But he couldn't do his work—he couldn't remember details. Eventually those brain cells revived and he could do his work again, but he wasn't normal. It was like he could sit fifteen minutes looking at his shoes, saying, "I have to put my shoes on." Of course, the shock treatments from those days caused a depression.

Abuse Grows as the Family Grows

During the years of increasing mental illness and abuse, we had our three daughters: Jade, Jasmine, and Jocelyn. As I struggled with raising three young children, the abuse just kept escalating until at last there was a break from the abusive pattern. Bill was on medication, and I think he really wanted to try. He believed that I meant it when I said I would call the cops if he ever touched me again. Though he refrained from the physical abuse, he turned to verbal abuse. And then he started to drink.

It was awful. Bill isolated us from family and friends. We would be friends with people, and all of a sudden they would do something to upset him and that was it. He would have me record conversations with them because he would tell me, "This is what I want you to tell them." And he would record conversations to see if I would do it. I was always trying to please him. Then I would begin to catch it again if I didn't do what he wanted me to do.

The physical abuse started again after nearly three years of no violence. A day came when he said to me that he was going to beat me with a strap. He said, "Go buy me a carton of cigarettes, and when you get home, you are going to get it."

I said, "Can I take the baby with me?"

He said, "Yes, and you better come back."

I called my brother-in-law and said, "I'm not going home. I'm going to school to pick up my other two daughters because he is going to kill me."

I went out to Hope House, which is a Catholic retreat house, and told the priest, "I can't go home; my husband has such anger. Can I stay here?"

He said, "You can't sleep here because we're having a retreat." But he allowed us to stay for the day. He said, "Does your husband know you're all right? I would like you to call him. Don't tell him where you are, but just let him know you are okay because you do have his baby with you."

I said, "Please, call my husband. You have to be in it to know how it is." When I called, I heard this inhuman screech; it sounded like demons. The priest took the phone from me, and he hung it up. That priest anointed my head with oil and prayed over me.

Because my brother-in-law decided to move into our home, I went back. He lived with us for a while because I was afraid to be alone with my husband. My brother-in-law saw my husband's behavior firsthand. But he thought I must have done a lot to provoke it. I was so taken aback, I said, "How can you think that? I'm not perfect, but how can you think I can provoke him to do these things?" So then I didn't even feel totally safe with my brother-in-law around for protection. Maybe he, too, thought I should "get it."

We were going for counseling. Bill had a psychiatrist and a psychologist. He would go to sessions and blame me for everything, saying, "My wife did this. My wife did that."

He continued to threaten to kill me. My fear was very great because something was beginning to change. One day he got the shotgun and shells and said, "I think I'll blast you one."

"Come on, that's ridiculous. The kids will walk in and what would they think?"

"Aren't you scared?" he asked.

"No, because I know you wouldn't do that." That was the first time he ever pulled the gun on me. But he was repentant afterward.

He hurt me again and we went to the hospital. He told them I was so terribly bruised because I'd fallen down the steps. When we got home, the kids were confused and crying, and I looked at him and said, "Do you see what you're doing to the kids?"

But then when he was gentle I would forget everything.

"FOR I KNOW THE PLANS I HAVE FOR YOU," DECLARES THE LORD, "PLANS TO PROSPER YOU AND NOT TO HARM YOU, PLANS TO GIVE YOU HOPE AND A FUTURE."

—JEREMIAH 29:11

There would be times when he really would sit with me and talk. For my tenth anniversary in 1985, my brother-in-law gave us a trip down to CBN to see Pat Robertson. Bill was happy to go. In that "normalcy part"— in the steady center of the bipolar disorder—there was that belief in God, that pursuit of God. Bill was going to try different churches, but I wasn't ready to go.

We moved again in 1987; things with Bill had been a little bit better. He got a promotion and a transfer to Chicago, and we bought a house. The first night we spent there, he kept threatening to kill me.

I said, "Why don't you just do it and get it over with?" I was so tired of the threats. I remember I walked downstairs, and he got back into bed; I didn't even go up to talk about it or think about it. Later, he came downstairs. I said, "Bill, we can't live this way. We just can't." But we did.

One morning the kids had to get ready for school, but I couldn't help them because the night before Bill had given me a black eye. So he got them ready. As they were coming in to say good-bye, I had the sheet pulled over part of my face to cover the damage. "Oh, Mommy, what's wrong?" asked my oldest daughter.

"Nothing."

Bill said, "Yes, you know what you did. The door was open; she went to get up and hit right into the door." And this is what he told the kids—the same kind of story all the time.

Our kids were in Christian school and Bill's condition had continued to deteriorate, but I saw enough of the good to hang in there, because there was that part of him I knew didn't want to be sick. I saw it when he tried; I saw it when he was really sorry. To the people on the outside, we looked like that family a lot of people would want to be, because when he was on medication, things were okay.

Then he started to drink again; he had stopped alcohol for almost seven years, and then he went back to it. He had also stopped smoking, and he started to smoke again. If he thought he saw somebody from the church and he was smoking in the car, he would be paranoid. Everything was hidden.

The physical abuse would go in spurts. He would call me at work: "You had better get home now, or else. If not, I'm coming there to get you." I would leave everything and go. He wouldn't let me go back to work that day. It wasn't always a beating, but there were threats all the time. They were always degrading.

In 1992 my husband stopped work completely. He called me from work, saying, "I feel like I'm going to put a chair through the window." I urged him to come home and he did. My husband had always fought accepting his emotional illness, but at that point, he began to embrace it: "After all, I'm sick! I can't help it. I'm sick!"

He went into a depression in which he was like a vegetable. It was wonderful! There was no abuse during that time. You know, it's terrible to say, but it was really wonderful.

Then he came out of his depression. We had changed churches and were now going to a very small, intimate church. Our Father in heaven knows exactly what He is doing. People knew each other at this church, and God put one girl there for me who said, "I see terror in your eyes." But we still didn't say anything to the church people.

As the depression lifted, Bill started to change, showing signs of sleep deprivation and bizarre behaviors. He would isolate me in the bedroom and scream at me for hours. And then he would say, "Okay, now I got to hit you!"

Later I found out my children, especially our middle child, Jasmine, would be in the bathroom listening at the door but too scared to go in. So Jasmine made believe she had an appendix attack to draw him away. Jade began to fake anxiety attacks. These kids were watching us, and they could see the abuse was getting more aggressive toward me, but they could lure him away, and this is what they were doing.

The Lord gave us Joshua 1:9—"Do not be terrified"—and they would huddle in the bathroom and say it because we were truly terrified.

My priority was to survive. I convinced myself the abuse wasn't touching them because he protected his daughters physically and verbally, but now he was isolating the children from me.

On paper he made a pyramid listing topics ranging from what a bad wife I was to what a bad mother I was. He wrote about how I did not defend him, how I was a coward, how I would protect others before I would protect him. There were ten subjects, and I had to make one-hour tapes. He would listen to them, and if I breathed too long, I would have to make the tape over. After I made these tapes, he made the children listen to them over and over. This was around 1996, when Jade was a senior in high school, Jasmine was fifteen, and Jocelyn was eleven. They would say to me, "Mommy, don't worry. We don't believe anything we have to listen to."

The Point of Separation

I know that I, too, had become mentally ill at the time—a complete basket case! Do you know what finally made me move out? I moved out of the house because he convinced me that I was the creator of all the trouble. It was *my* fault! I decided to look for a little apartment and have the girls visit me because I truly believed I had created all this turmoil. I thought I was making him enraged and my children would be better off if I was not there. When I would visit with them, everything would be okay, I believed. I now understand that was exactly what he wanted, so he would have the children to himself to turn against me. Somewhere down the line, he began to truly hate me in those last years.

THE LORD YOUR GOD IS WITH YOU, HE IS MIGHTY TO SAVE. HE WILL TAKE GREAT DELIGHT IN YOU, HE WILL QUIET YOU WITH HIS LOVE, HE WILL REJOICE OVER YOU WITH SINGING.

—ZEPHANIAH 3:17

We separated in 1997. I read a book that talked about being a victim no longer and said, "That's *me!* That's it! Enough is enough!"

One day I went home to visit my children. Bill was lying on the couch, and the children were sitting there, and they were all crying. When I walked in, I said, "Bill, why are the kids crying?"

He said in a twisted voice, "They felt very sorry for me," but it was literally like a demon's voice.

I said, "I am not leaving here. I am staying. I am not going anyplace without the girls."

It became a sort of forty-eight-hour hostage experience. He wouldn't allow us to eat at all the first day or talk to each other. And he kept us inside two days and two nights. The kids couldn't go to school, and I couldn't go to work. It was horrible. He had my children downstairs, and I had to stay at the top of the stairs. I heard him tell my Jasmine, "If you don't stay with me, I will gouge your eyes out."

He was threatening the children, so I sneaked to a phone to call my pastor. I told him and the elders what was happening. This was the first time I ever told my church about Bill.

It was such a huge step for me to get that help. I know God spoke to me and said, "Now!" He spoke so clearly I knew if I didn't act I would be in total disobedience to Him. So I called for help.

The pastor and the elders came at six in the morning. I called Bill's brother at work and said, "My pastor is coming. We are getting out. Bill is dangerous." They scooped us out, then stayed at my house until Bill woke up about eleven in the morning. There were the pastor, three elders, and his brother. He managed to keep them captivated with his smooth talk for about eight or nine hours.

They said to him, "Bill, you said earlier today that you were going to move; that's the best thing to do. So we are asking you now, for the sake of your wife and the kids, to move out."

He said, "I'm not going anywhere. I *may* have said the best thing would be if I moved out, but I am not going to do it."

The children and I went to my pastor's house and stayed there. He had four little kids and a sweet wife, God bless her. I remember saying to him, "We have nowhere to go." I had totally alienated my own family to please Bill. Our pastor and his wife welcomed us in.

Not knowing any better, I didn't move my clothes or anything. We stayed a few weeks there, going back and forth to the house to get things. I didn't know what else to do, so I made phone calls to search for a "safe house," but none of them had four beds. They wanted to split us up. I said, "Absolutely not." I knew I had to do it God's way, and the system wouldn't do it God's way.

We couldn't stop Bill from coming to the house because we didn't know what our legal rights were. He began to talk to the kids outside, and I would listen by the window. All of a sudden Jade came in and said, "Mommy, I want to go home and stay with Daddy. He's all by himself. He'll be okay."

"You are *not* going with Daddy."

"Mommy, please, come on! He's all by himself. He's crying. He feels bad."

I said, "If anybody goes, we will all go." So I held him off for a couple of days, and he would come every day, crying and what not. I wasn't strong enough yet. I didn't know my legal rights. I didn't know anything. Finally we all went back. That was the worst hell we ever lived through.

We were only back for a week. It got so bad that I sent Jade and Jasmine to camp to get them out of the house. He let them go. He figured he could control little Jocelyn and me. The camp called two days later saying Jasmine was not feeling well, not adjusting. Actually, she was petrified about what was going on back home. So I had to get her. Jocelyn and Bill and I drove together to pick up Jasmine. When we got to her she said, "Daddy, I just want to come home. I want to come home."

He took Jade for a walk by himself and asked if she wanted to come back home. But she wanted to stay at the camp. I don't remember the ride home, to be honest with you. The next two or three days, whatever was left of that week, were horrible. It was like after we left, all the abuse came back stronger.

While Bill was at the psychiatrist's office with Jocelyn, Jasmine had a panic attack. I knew I had to get her out of the house, and with my pastor's help, I did. But Jade chose to stay. Later I learned she would not live with me because she was petrified that I would not be able to protect her from Bill. I filed an order of protection against my husband and separated from him again.

It took two months to get custody of Jocelyn and Jasmine. During that time Bill told Jocelyn, "If you talk to your mother, I will divorce her." She was only eleven years old. It was very traumatic. Bill started beating Jade, so she went to live with his brother and sister before she went to college.

There was a time when Bill would write me threatening letters. The police thought he was going to come and kill me on Mother's Day, because he kept saying, "Two weeks left." We went to a town thirty minutes away, but we didn't stay there.

My husband took my name off all the accounts. He had done well working for a big company, and he withdrew nearly half a million dollars from retirement and other accounts. Nothing was left. He stole my car because he said it was in his name. So I had no clothes—nothing. He was in the house we left, so I had to find a small place to rent. It was $750 a month, which was just a little less than my income at the school. We made it look decent and lived there for the three years after I was separated. God's provision came. There was food left for us on the steps. My niece gave us a car. You know, God was just wonderful.

I had to keep an alarm system set in my small house for the three years I lived there because of his constant threats. He also had an investigator follow Jocelyn and me, and she was petrified. I was able to gain custody of Jocelyn because of a legal error. Bill's lawyer took testimony from Jocelyn, which was illegal because she was underage. So that was

God's hand intervening. And then at the end when they gave me final custody, Bill had no custody, no visitation. Jocelyn wrote a letter to the judge that said, "Judge, I love my dad, but he scares me. I know he is going to feel bad, but I don't want to visit with him because I am afraid, but I love my dad."

The judge told Bill, "We know Jocelyn loves you, but she's afraid of you. It is our decision that she not visit with you, but she wants you to know she loves you." My husband went ballistic in court, while I was just sitting there, praying. The judge looked at me and gave me a wink. I saw what God was doing and couldn't believe it. So I got full custody of our youngest daughter, Jocelyn, with no visitation at all by Bill.

So into 1997 we lived in the little house. We really didn't hear much from him or see him because we had all this legal protection and he wanted to keep his corporate position.

An End to the Torment

Bill was killed in June 1997. There was a lot of demonic stuff at the end. It was like he just opened himself up to the darkness. When the two plainclothes policemen came to my house that Friday at midnight, I was so scared until they showed me their badges. They came in, sat down, and said, "It's about your husband."

I was shaken. "Where is he?"

"He's been killed in a shoot-out with police officers."

I felt total disbelief and relief at the very same time. It was just two days before Jasmine graduated from high school.

When I went back to the house, I saw clues about what had been happening there. The side door was nailed shut; every window had blankets over it. Yet, the kids' rooms were untouched. The night he was killed, he had been drinking with the man next door, and eventually the police were called. They were trying to talk to Bill from the porch. He got his shotgun as a police officer was trying to come in through the front door. They told him, "Put your hands on the screen," and then they tried to grab his hands through the screen. He pulled away and threatened to shoot the officer who broke through the front door. During the confrontation, Bill was shot.

My oldest daughter Jade moved back immediately. She had clearly stayed with my in-laws for those two years to ensure protection for all of us. What a tragedy for her life.

When Bill died, the IRS wanted back taxes paid. Bill had received bad advice from his attorney and never paid taxes on all his earnings. We found out there was $106,000 of debt I was liable for. I knew I'd have to pay it. We went to see the IRS. The man who was handling the case was kind and said, "I am sorry about this."

I said, "I want to know how I can repay this. I'm trying to sell the house, but I'd like to know if I can get at least half from the sale of the house so I have money to buy something for us to live in."

"Okay, let me see." He went to the back office for a while and then came around the counter with news that was beyond unbelievable. I left, drove halfway home, and then went back because I thought, *This can't be real!* I was exonerated by the Internal Revenue Service for the $106,000.

But God! But God! O God! Wow God! How God? Thank you, sweet Jesus!

We cleaned out the house. I asked the kids if they wanted to live there and start over. All three voted no—*NO!* So we sold it, and I was able to buy this townhouse.

God's hand of protection was evident in the wake of Bill's

death. Bill and I were never even legally separated—which means the divorce never came about. I was his widow, and as his widow I was entitled to his pension benefits and to other things. So all the time God kept intervening. There were things that had occurred that, at the time, I hadn't understood. But God has His plans, and we were cared for financially as a result.

Reflections on God's Care in the Battlefield

Serena says the most important thing to be gained from her story is the reality that though there is sorrow in her heart, there is no bitterness, no unforgiveness. Yes, when she thinks now of some of the terrible events, she may feel anger, but forgiveness still comes.

She has had to forgive herself for the things she didn't do, steps she didn't take as her husband's abuse turned her into what she calls a basket case who was just existing, just trying to survive. She aches for her daughters, saying, "I can see clearly now when I think of things concerning the kids; it hurts. I have honestly repented to the Lord for not doing anything about it, for allowing Bill to do what he did for as long as he did."

Being married to a mentally ill person is never easy. Serena advises a person in that situation to keep her eyes open and not be afraid of the truth. Dealing with anyone who is consistently in any emotional state is going to be a scary roller coaster. Just living with someone who is on that roller coaster, with emotional ups and downs, affects *everything*. Serena doesn't believe medication alone is the answer. "What you really need is psychological help and spiritual accountability. That is the easy thing, to medicate. And it doesn't end. It seems that it progresses as you get older because the stronghold gets stronger."

What about the aspect of being a Christian in such a marriage? Serena says to remove yourself from the situation, though not necessarily through divorce: "Let God deal with you on that. You have to remove yourself. There is Scripture that helped me so much. It is in *The Amplified Bible,* Malachi 2:16: 'For the Lord, the God of Israel, says: "I hate divorce and marital separation and him who covers his garment [his wife] with violence. Therefore keep a watch upon your spirit [that it may be controlled by My Spirit], that you deal not treacherously and faithlessly [with your marriage mate]."' When we were separated, I was very upset. I didn't want to do what God didn't want me to do. I was so afraid of being disobedient that I got the elders of my church involved. I came to understand that God does not want me in a marital relationship experiencing violence.

"That is what released me to say, 'Lord, I know in Your eyes I am okay, because at the end, You will be my driving force.' I did get different advice from different Christians. There were Christians saying, 'We'll get the car. We'll break into the house, grab the kids, and go.' The Lord said to me, 'No! You will move in righteousness.' And that seemed like the path I should take.

"A pastor came to me and said, 'You are building walls instead of breaking them.' He tried to tell me what to do, but I had to tell him, this loving pastor, 'I can't. I know what God has told me. I have to stand on what I believe.' I got so much advice from people, but I needed to know what God wanted. Those are the things that so overshadow the opinions of others; there is no comparison."

Serena shared her words of hard-won wisdom with anyone who is encountering abuse. "Don't believe a lie. Get help, because it is there. If you are fearful, know that no matter what the threat is, you can be protected."

It may be hard not to feel as Serena did—that you are

hanging on by your fingernails, bound up by distorted thinking into taking no action, just praying it through. Serena said, "In spite of everything, I still had to take that step. He intervened to a point of urging me to leave, but I still ultimately had to take that step. I thank God that I was at that point in my life, too, because of my kids. In principle, they should have been all over the streets, in all kinds of messes, but God's protection was there, even for that."

Because of her personal experiences, Serena has taken every opportunity to tell her daughters what a healthy marriage and relationship *should* be. She promised them, "If I have reservations about the men you might marry, if I think there is anything wrong, I will tell you. Don't think marriage solves everything. I was a three-sided square who thought marriage would make me four-sided, but I was even lonelier in my marriage because it was the wrong thing.

"Thankfully, God has brought healthy, godly men into their lives."

And what is her greatest blessing today? "God blessed me with three wonderful girls. That is my abundant blessing out of all of this. That is my greatest testimony."

Serena's oldest daughter, Jade, graduated three years ago with a degree in business administration and is climbing the corporate ladder. She is fun loving and has forgiven her father. Jasmine, the middle daughter, is now married to an easygoing, loving Christian man, a husband that Serena says she would have chosen personally. The baby of the family, Jocelyn, teaches autistic children and is dating a young man who has just accepted the Lord.

Said Serena, "They really are just a blessing. As any mother who knows the Lord would say, my desire is that my children will walk in His ways, and they are—thank God. They went through their struggles with forgiveness, but my girls are home. That is another miracle—it was God's protection for them. They also are a powerful witness to my family and to friends and neighbors because many think or say, 'These kids should have been on the streets.' We just thank God; there is no denying His protection and provision. He is such an awesome God!

"The beauty of it is that my other relatives see the evidence of God in my life. At a family member's funeral, my nephew said, 'Aunt Serena, how are you doing?' When I said I was doing fine, he answered, 'You are the strong one in the family.' This is a testimony of what God has done in somebody's life. And they know it! They know because God has changed me. I had to depend on God so much to raise my children in that terrible situation; they could see that."

HOW PRICELESS IS YOUR UNFAILING LOVE! BOTH HIGH AND LOW AMONG MEN FIND REFUGE IN THE SHADOW OF YOUR WINGS.

—PSALM 36:7

I asked Serena what she wished she knew a long time ago, and she answered without hesitation: "My value." Is she now embracing her role as a daughter of the King? Yes, today she realizes that she has unlimited worth. She is truly a princess.

"I know I am so valuable to my Father in heaven. I know He rejoices over me. I know He knows every thought I think, what I could bear. I know He stuck with me and never let me go all those times. When I was unfaithful, He was so faithful. I keep thinking of that song lyric, 'Because He lives, I can face tomorrow,' because sometimes I didn't want to face tomorrow. I didn't think there would be a tomorrow! And now there is another song: 'Lord, I offer my life to You, everything I've been through. Use it for Your glory.'

"I can truly say, 'Lord, if what I have gone through can help someone else to know there's hope, then let me help them.' There is a way out. There is a God who loves you and will bear with you even when you ask, 'Where are You?' He has the perfect plan for your life."

In spite of all she has been through, is she still "No Sweat Serena"?

She says with that shy smile, "If you need anything, yes. I'll be there for you. But that's just me. I thank God for that."

When we hurt, it forces us
to embrace God out of urgent,
desperate need. God is never
closer than when your
heart is aching.

—Joni Eareckson Tada

CHAPTER SIX

Tracy: Knowing Joy Comes in the Morning

I met with Tracy in a hotel room in Tulsa. A friend of mine heard her speak at church, then recommended I consider her story for the book. Tracy sent a tape ahead of time, and I was fairly glued to the testimony of her life.

Tracy arrived at our interview with an older woman who is one of her mentors. Knowing the tragedy she has faced and the heavy responsibilities she carries, I expected to meet a woman with a bit of a sullen spirit. What I saw in Tracy's eyes was not sadness as much as seriousness. She is tall, thin, beautifully coiffed, and lovely … almost porcelain. Her posture was erect, her manner refined and gentle, if not reserved. I asked Tracy to share a bit about her life before marriage.

IN HER OWN WORDS: TRACY'S STORY

I grew up in a middle-class, solid Christian home, very active in my church. It's all I knew. It was my favorite place to be. I went off to college and studied elementary education there. All I ever wanted to be was married, a mom, and a wife. My parents said I would never find anyone to meet my standards, but I knew God had someone really special in mind.

I didn't date a lot, partly because there wasn't anyone I wanted to date. I wasn't the prettiest or the most popular. I was just your average girl.

My heart was really toward the Lord. I just had this very high standard, even when I got out of college. I dated one guy in college and he just wasn't right. It was a big disappointment to be graduating and not to be getting married. That was the scary thing because I really didn't want a career. When I was in high school, I believed, on one hand, I would eventually marry a pastor. On the other hand, I always felt like the right guy would not be out there, and then, even if he *was* out there, I would somehow not meet his standards. At times I'd think, *God is saving me someone, my real Prince Charming, and he's going to ride in on a white horse and I'll have the fairy-tale wedding.*

Then I met Rick. He was in a Christian band and I attended a concert—someone was trying to fix me up with him. I was excited, but when I first met him, I had a judgmental thing going on because he had really long hair and wore shorts at an evening concert. But he was very, very cute. And yeah, there is something dumb about it, that you meet a guy and get married nine months later. I really felt that he was the one God wanted me to marry.

When we met after that first concert, I was very judgmental; *he's cute, good-looking, and my, can he sing! He can't possibly love God if he's all of that. He can't really have a heart for the Lord.* But all he really wanted to talk about was his relationship with the Lord, his walk with the Lord. And that's what was so impressive to me because that's what I really wanted—a man whose heart was toward the Lord.

Rick called the next morning. He said, "I told the Lord, 'If You let me marry her, I'd be the happiest man in the world.'"

I went home and told my roommate I felt I'd met the man I was going to marry. That's how we started off the relationship, telling each other we knew we were meant for one another. And so when he came back, it was July. He came back again in August on vacation—to get to know the woman he was going to marry. That was the goal of spending his vacation near my parents' home in Tulsa. So we entered into a courtship. Courtship, for many Christians, is to move toward marriage without the "trial dating" roller coaster. It is a mutual agreement that says, *you are the one*. I did, at one time, embrace the courtship philosophy.

Still, there were some red flags at the beginning. In the first letter he wrote me, he was so desperate to be honest and real. He had a reputation for not being honest or genuine; he was the only single guy in the band and was known as the playboy. He was the one who would woo the crowds, and he was put at center stage for that purpose. Their hearts weren't doing that in a wrong way; it just made good sense since Rick was so handsome and charismatic. He had a pretty wild past, but he really had turned to the Lord and sincerely desired to live a godly life. So he decided not to keep anything secret from me.

I was working for a Christian speaker at that time, and my boss called Rick because he knew Rick and the guys in the band. This godly gentleman was a very protective force in my life. I didn't know he'd done this until later, but he called and said, "Rick, if you're going to marry Tracy, you must tell her everything she needs to know about you." I later learned that everybody else knew about Rick. All I knew was that he was talented, attractive, and had a heart for the Lord. So in Rick's first letter, he did tell me all about his past. He told me he tried to commit suicide when he was in junior high. He told me he thought he had gotten a girl pregnant. And that was the greatest fear of his life. I can still remember reading that

THOSE WHO KNOW
YOUR NAME WILL
TRUST IN YOU,
FOR YOU, LORD,
HAVE NEVER
FORSAKEN THOSE
WHO SEEK YOU.

—PSALM 9:10

letter and just crying and thinking, *Lord, I really felt like I was to marry a virgin man.*

I didn't tell anyone I'd gotten that letter, so I really worked through it with the Lord. It was hard to accept because I felt I was to get a virgin prize, since I had "saved" myself. Yet, the old is passed away, and he still seemed to be the one God wanted me to marry. I felt like Gomer in Scripture; it seemed God was saying, "You're going to start this out with forgiveness." So I had to start with forgiveness and work through that. Now I can't say for sure it was God's voice. My desire was to marry Rick. Sometimes I just have to say the Lord gave me the desire of my heart. Whether that was really His perfect plan, I'll never know.

I was such a virgin—mentally, emotionally, in every way. I can still remember the first kiss. It was very aggressive, almost intrusive. Was there anything in his behavior from that time that I can look back on and see the direction he was going? I didn't, because I took it as flattery. I was going to meet his every single physical need and be everything he wanted. I do remember the night before we got married, he called me and said, "I can't wait to get married. I won't ever have to masturbate again." I honestly didn't even really know what he was saying. I didn't know what masturbation was. But that was his addiction. That was from the "I'm your best friend; I love you; I want to tell you *everything* there is to know about me" part of his personality. And he really felt like I was going to take that addiction away; he reasoned he had the addiction because he didn't have a wife. That was flattering, and I didn't have the wisdom or self-confidence to realize what he was really saying to me. I see now that he was crying out at that point.

Tracy's Anorexia

I'd been single for so long, it was strange to have the accountability of Rick saying, "That is not a normal plate of food. You *have* to eat." He would travel all the time with the band, so he would call me and ask, "What did you have to eat?" And I wouldn't lie. So I was put in intensive treatment. In helping me to become free, he realized, "Oh, *I've* got an addiction, too. I've got the same or similar thing going on. I'm powerless over a habit, a mind-set. I'm addicted to masturbation and pornography." As a bride of only four months, I'm thinking, *You have got to be kidding me.* It was so devastating.

Two people in bondage have linked up, thinking the marriage would free us, but only the Lord would take us out of bondage. My anorexia had actually started during my teenage years, and it became full blown in college when I was living with roommates who were competitive in appearance and in every other way. Anorexia is such a perfection/performance-driven kind of thing. I really didn't want to be anorexic, but I really did want to be thin. I was already very thin. That's the sick part of it.

I made it through high school and college, and my health did not fail. I thought I could control the anorexia, but I was actually out of control. It really got bad right after college, when I began my teaching career. There were no roommates, nobody to blame, and I would get home for dinner and my dad would say, "That's all you're going to eat?" They started picking up on it.

> FOR YOU CREATED MY INMOST BEING; YOU KNIT ME TOGETHER IN MY MOTHER'S WOMB.... MY FRAME WAS NOT HIDDEN FROM YOU WHEN I WAS MADE IN THE SECRET PLACE. WHEN I WAS WOVEN TOGETHER IN THE DEPTHS OF THE EARTH, YOUR EYES SAW MY UNFORMED BODY. ALL THE DAYS ORDAINED FOR ME WERE WRITTEN IN YOUR BOOK BEFORE ONE OF THEM CAME TO BE.
>
> —PSALM 139:13, 15–16

As for the loved ones who watch our demise, they are in a no-win situation. Don't say, "Is that all you're going to eat?" because it makes us want to say, "Yeah, that's *all* I'm going to eat; what are you going to do about it?" An anorexic person will always fight back. It's a control thing, and if they don't say anything, then we're thinking, *Oh, they're not noticing me. I don't matter and I look fat.* It's just a vicious, evil, wicked thing that I'm free of. God really used that to allow me to walk where I am today, depending on Him and having more of an understanding of what my husband's struggle was.

The morning after the wedding, Rick asked me if I thought we had made a mistake. That was really devastating to me. It was the very next morning after we had this big, fairy-tale wedding. And I thought I was riding off into the sunset to live happily ever after. He rolled over in bed and he seriously asked, "Do think we made a mistake?"

I was thinking, *What in the world? We can't undo this. We can't undo this because I'm committed now.* It was the beginning of what he would do to me throughout our marriage—the Dr. Jekyll and Mr. Hyde syndrome—*I just married you, but will you just be my best friend for a few minutes and let me confide in you that I think we made a mistake?* What he was *really* saying, now that I understand addiction, was, "I thought this new physical thing was going to change everything going on in my mind and everything going on in my heart. And I'm waking up with the same lustful fantasies and thoughts. It didn't go away overnight because I got married." And of course, again I was thinking, *I can't do anything about this now.* It was such a lonely feeling. Very scary. I had everything going for me, and I'd left it all to go off and be his wife. Now he thought I might be a mistake. No one had ever told me before that talking to me or being around me felt like a mistake. And now I was with someone who thought *marrying* me was a mistake!

It was really devastating. This was not what I had pictured. Of course, I didn't know what I should be picturing because I was so sheltered. But then later he would come along and have this other tender side. It just started out as Jekyll and Hyde. It really did.

As I look back over the last fifteen years, I'm not sure that I'd say Rick was bipolar or had a split personality. I do know that the Enemy came and mocked me then. Just before we got married, Rick was really into reading these (good) books on Christian marriage and seemed to be getting prepared. He was trying to build himself up in a healthy sense. I had no idea of his unhealthy past. He was determined to be this godly Christian man. All he had ever known was lust and pornography, and he thought he would do it "right" this time. But the flesh is weak. Instead of going to God to show him how to be the right man, he was trying to do outward things to be the right man. He almost missed the wedding because he made a family member go back to get his robe because he told people he wanted to have his robe on for the first night. It all sounded so sweet and impressive. But it was a show— or at least a smoke screen. He was fighting such a controlling power of lust that he actually had no control whatsoever.

That part of it was just a shock. The honeymoon was horrible.

From that point on, it was like, "We'll just be room-mates—you'll be my friend." And we made great roommates. But that was just not acceptable. I didn't want to be his room-mate. We were married! Thankfully, there was some laughter. I was laughing on the outside, crying on the inside. He did care for me. He was my best friend. And God used him to bring me freedom from my own addiction. Rick's mission became getting me healed from anorexia.

He'd say, "We need to focus on *your* problem. *Your* prob-lem is a matter of life and death; mine is not." He wasn't even in tune with his issues until I went through mine. And then it wasn't like he really wanted healing. He was actually just able to begin to understand, and to think, *Oh, wow, maybe I'm out of control too.*

My anorexia came to my attention because it came to his attention. My parents had been aware of it, so they had prob-ably been talking to him. I was not aware that it had so much control over me. Rick would come off the road and fix a plate of food. And I would think *I couldn't eat that portion over a whole month!* He just suggested, "Why don't we go see if you need some help?" I actually had the mind-set that I would prove him wrong, that I didn't have anorexia. Inside, though,

I was crying out, wanting help. The real sickness would have been to return to believing I didn't need any help.

We went for a diagnosis, and they said I had full-fledged anorexia. They wanted to treat me immediately and admit me to an intensive twenty-eight-day program. I was thinking this was a waste of time and money. I was feeling really stupid, asking myself, *What's the problem? I just don't want to be fat.* Well, it's a big problem if it's driving your whole life. I guess they figured it was as good a time as any. When they said, "Do you realize you'll probably never have children?" that was the tipping point, the main motive to check it out because I really, really wanted children. And I told myself the whole time I was there that God wanted me to be an evangelist. I was there to help everyone else come to know the Lord. I rationalized it was all about *them*, not about me.

I didn't have to spend the night. It was near Tulsa, but because I lived there, it was cheaper and more convenient to live at home. I had to be there at eight in the morning, but I was actually there by seven (more perfection). I ate three meals and left every night at eleven.

At home, Rick was gone most of the time. It was the peak of the band's travel schedule. I went home just to sleep. We had to show up at the center for breakfast. We had to document what we ate. They would watch us eat. We would weigh in. They would bring these big platters of food. It was comical. There were ten to fifteen of us. We would eat, and then someone would ask, "How did you feel about what you just ate?" The answers were always the same the first few days: "I feel fat." So the whole time I was thinking, *I cannot believe I'm in this place.*

Some people were eating their hair, and others were admitted for eating pencils. There was some real demonic stuff. And you have some who are so controlling they refuse to hear anything about the Lord. We had these rap (discussion) groups, and we were not talking about food. I'm saying, "This is all about food." And they're saying, "This is *so not* all about food. It's about being wounded in your childhood." You have to dig things up and remember everything you ever experienced, from bumping your knee to your mom saying something mean. And you're thinking, *This is why I don't eat?* It was really intense.

I had suffered for years, and now things could get better in just twenty-eight days. It seems a long time when you're there, but when you get out, you sort of miss the security. I knew I was going to be safe there. They guaranteed me I would not be fat. It was just like learning to walk. I knew I wanted to keep eating because I hadn't gotten fat and I did feel good—and wow, this is good. But you've got to keep at it when you're out of a program. So I have been. I test the waters here and there. Can I go without a meal here and there? No, I can't really do that. The Lord has been so faithful to me. Rick was my biggest cheerleader. I continue to this day to make myself accountable because I've got seven kids who know my story. "Are you sure that's all you're going to eat, Mommy?" I don't ever want to go back there. I found out I like eating. It's okay to eat, and I can say with integrity that I am walking in freedom today.

We had our first child two years after we married. And every fifteen months after that we had another baby. As with any marriage, babies and pregnancies affect intimacy. Rick was always trying so hard. I would say, "I just want to be appealing to you. I want to be seductive to you as your wife." But it was never like that. It was like he had to work up to being intimate. He tried. I could tell he was awkward in what should have been natural. We would get into bed, and he would just talk for hours to avoid being intimate. He'd always masturbated earlier and didn't need me, but he knew I needed him. Women like to communicate verbally, but it was a role reversal—really odd. I would always feel like I was going crazy. And he was so good at denial. He was "onstage" in our bedroom conversations. He insisted we were doing just fine, that we were happy roommates, and that this is how all normal marriages are. I would never blame the kids for distracting us, but life got really, really busy. I had four babies in four years, and he was traveling and singing eighteen days a month. After baby number four is when he had his first affair.

I know it was his first because Rick was also my best friend. And he said, "I'm going to hurt you. But I'm going to be the first to tell you that I hurt you. I'm not going to let anyone else tell you before I get to tell you because more than anything else, we're true friends." He's confessed to two, but I would never be surprised if there were more. I don't go there. I don't have any reason to.

After the wedding, he told me graphically about every encounter he had before our marriage. I would sit there and think, *Why is he telling me this?* Some stories he would tell more than once, almost as a cry for help.

I didn't see the red flags. Well, I didn't *want* to see the red flags. I wanted to be married and was attracted to Rick physically and spiritually, and I have since faced many consequences that are still very present.

To this day, there is still a tendency to return to past behaviors. Addicts understand this well. That's the thorn in my flesh. I have to make a choice every day to walk in freedom, meal by meal. I don't really want to be in bondage to food, but I still don't want to be fat. So I walk with boundaries. But it's easier to walk within food boundaries. Sexual boundaries are a lot harder to walk within this day and age.

And there was no one we knew of that could help. He went to my counselor at my eating treatment center and said, "Do you help people who are addicted to masturbation and pornography?" And I'm thinking, *I can't even say the M-word.* They wouldn't even call sex an addiction. It wasn't until he left the Christian band that he could hear me say, "Rick, you are addicted to sex." I thought I was making up a whole new term. I had never heard it before. And he would say, "You know what, I think that's exactly what it is."

We finally found a doctor. To appease me, Rick said, "Okay, I'll go to the doctor and tell him I'm in bondage and need to be free." But he wasn't willing to work at that. It was the old Jekyll and Hyde pattern. He really did want to be a good husband, but he did not submit to authority or accountability.

There was a friend with whom I went to treatment, and I shared the situation with her. Amazingly, her husband was also addicted to masturbation and pornography—I thought I was telling her something no one had ever heard of—so we would confide in each other. And I never told anyone else, because I was his best friend and a faithful wife.

My friend was relieved to know she wasn't alone, but we didn't really know what to do. We shared our war stories back and forth, but it led to nothing. The band headed out to five more cities, and I got busy with the kids. I kind of pushed it away, telling myself, *It's going to get better, and it's not really as bad as I'm making it out to be. He is a good dad, a good husband, so I can live with this.*

He so desperately wanted to be free. He threatened suicide the first seven years of our marriage, and he feared the possibility of adultery. I concluded, "I'm either going to wind up with a dead husband, or one who's not faithful to me."

Rick would be crying on the floor and doing this big drama thing. I would think, *Wow, I don't even know how to begin to help him.* And there I was ignorantly trying to help him while he was hurting me.

Remember, we were "best friends," so he wanted to let me know he was afraid of hurting me. That's why when he came and confessed the first affair, it was the realization of one of my greatest fears. My greatest recurring fear/nightmare was whether or not he would ever commit suicide.

We had four kids and had been married six years. The affair happened in March, and he confessed it in May. It was so dramatic. He held it in for eight weeks, and I was clueless about it. He came home literally crawling up the driveway. He called me after a concert and said, "I'm sick and I'm coming home." It was 1:30 in the morning when he arrived. As I waited for him to get home, the Lord told me very gently and clearly that Rick was coming home to confirm that one of my greatest fears had become a reality. I knew—I just knew. His best pal at the time was the one who made him go home, and he told me Rick was suicidal. He said if he hadn't driven Rick home, he believes Rick would have killed himself that night.

It was horrible. I just went numb. I locked up. I had four babies under the age of four. I remember burning everything in the kitchen. I couldn't cook. I would even burn water. The anger was so intense; the pain was so intense. It was a wicked time of grief during those first hours and days. It was a Friday I found out, and by Sunday morning, I said, "I'm going to church and I'm going by myself." By then, I was calling the shots. "You've messed up, buddy. I'm going to be in control from now on. You're staying home with the kids." That had never happened before because Rick was not usually home on Sunday mornings. I would wash and dress all the little toddlers, get them in their car seats, and get them all to their Sunday school classes. Going to church was like a triathlon.

I knew I needed to go that Sunday morning and to be alone. There was a guest preacher who singled me out and said he sensed I was going through some hard things that only God knew. He told me I was in "transition." I almost laughed and wanted to say, "Buddy, we are definitely in transition. And it had better be for a good purpose!" Of course, I didn't.

On the way to church that morning I said, "God, I've got to hear from You. I have trusted You, have prayed for this man, and have begged for this not to happen. It's happened! So now, what are You going to do with all of it?"

The man with the word of encouragement told me this transition would be for "your good and God's glory." I obviously clung to that. I remember going home and telling my husband there's hope, and that God was going to use this for our good and His glory. Rick came back with me to church that night, because now he was desperate. He seemed to be feeling, *Okay, I've messed up. I've blown it. I'm repenting. How do I do this? How do we walk through this together?*

The summer passed, and still Rick did not tell the band. All the while, he was still touring. Counsel was given to us that we really needed to address the group ourselves before gossip spread. It was late September when he went to address the band and management. He confessed to them, and they gave him a six-week sabbatical. He was very broken and they were shocked. At the end of the sabbatical, they asked him to leave the ministry. It wasn't a surprise to him or me. But it wasn't what Rick wanted. He would never admit that. The band was his life: singing and touring, being front and center, being admired. It was all he ever wanted to do, but it all crumbled under him. Our fifth baby was born, and he was out of work.

When the Spotlight Went Out

Rick started a home business and really began to flounder. He was not a go-getter type. The band was the best thing for him because they told them where to be and when and what to do. Our finances were now in big trouble. At that point, very few people knew about the affair. The band knew, and to their credit they never shared it. They were gracious in making the transition smooth for our family. Only a few close friends knew, not even family.

Our parents were giving us such grief: "You've got five kids, and he just quits his job and starts a home business?" That didn't make sense, so we were finally pressured into telling them. We had five children under the age of five, no job, no insurance, and a home business with a man who was not motivated to sell. It was really scary, but God was so faithful. We didn't miss a meal. We didn't miss a bill. What a faithful Father and Provider Jesus is.

Rick was a great dad during that time, very connected. He loved the kids and they loved him. He lasted a few years going the home-business route. Being at poverty level with five children was probably harder than working through the affair. It was so painful. But we ate. I baked bread and had buckets of wheat and we would live on bread and beans. It was pretty horrible, but I tried not to be bitter. We never went into debt. Never. We lived within our means and we trusted God. Someone literally paid our house payments. It wasn't always the same person, though after the first year, the Lord raised up a family who paid our house payment consistently.

Eating beans every day didn't bother him as much as it was bothering me. There were a couple Christmases when I announced we would not be exchanging gifts. Our families couldn't let that go, and they would buy pretty much everything. It was so hard because I had been a teacher and I knew I could get out there and make some money. When we had seven children, I did finally say, "I guess I'm going out to work." I knew I could make more money than he could. "Anything you can do, I can do better" was the stage

DO NOT BE ANXIOUS ABOUT ANYTHING, BUT IN EVERYTHING, BY PRAYER AND PETITION, WITH THANKSGIVING, PRESENT YOUR REQUESTS TO GOD. AND THE PEACE OF GOD, WHICH TRANSCENDS ALL UNDERSTANDING, WILL GUARD YOUR HEARTS AND YOUR MINDS IN CHRIST JESUS.

—PHILIPPIANS 4:6–7

I was in. I can raise seven kids. I can handle this husband. I can go to work. I can do it all. I might end up in the hospital, but I was ready to do whatever it was going to take.

I have a controlling personality. It's a problem that led to the anorexia, and that's why I truly surrendered during all those home business years. We got into a new church, and this turned things around. The pastor took Rick aside and said, "What do you mean you're doing a home business? With seven kids? You don't have the personality for a home business. Shut the home business down and get a job! You do whatever it takes to bring in an income for this family." Rick listened to him. It was the first time Rick ever obeyed someone. He went to work for the county and pumped gas at night. He was working eighty hours a week. That ended up being the best thing that ever happened to us. You wouldn't think that having your husband working eighty hours a week was a good thing, but he had structure and less time on his hands for detours.

He never talked about missing the band or touring. He just kept saying the Lord would sustain us. He clung to that. I would ask, "Do you miss singing?" He insisted it was time for that season to be over. A new church life can be a blessing; there were no rumors and he was respected for being very talented. He eventually became the worship leader. Some people just need a new start.

During the eighty-hour workweek, I was virtually a single parent. Even when he had toured, from day one when I started having kids, he was always gone. He was such an onstage person, it worked well for him with the kids. When Daddy was home, he was determined to be super-daddy for an entire hour. He was on, animated, charming with the girls, funny with the boys. He loved the kids and they were his favorite topic with people. But he kind of pulled them out of the box and played with them and put them back when he decided time was up.

We were living in a fourteen-hundred square-foot house, but we weren't in any debt. Brighter days started to come. God gave us a home beyond our means when we were still at the same poverty level, and that home was twice the size. Rick was still working eighty hours a week when an old friend gave him a job at a large Fortune 500 company. We were pinching ourselves over his new salary that was actually going to meet our needs with a forty- to fifty-hour workweek. It was too good to be true.

The new job actually opened the door for Rick's addiction to resume with full force. He was no longer tired and had a lot more free time. He had spending money, less stress, and idle time to play. I had no clue what was coming around the corner. I really never dreamed he would go back toward that oppression and bondage or that he would ever want to walk that road again after all the pain he'd gone through, all the sacrifices. But it was his choice; he was once again out of control.

By then, there was really no physical relationship—we would go six months to a year. The sad joke was that because we had seven children, people thought we were in bed all the time. I conceived easily, once every fifteen months. I looked good, the wife married to a good-looking, talented guy. I was living a lie, hurting very badly. I was part of his lie of doing the right thing, having a great relationship, having all those babies. I wasn't able to share with anyone. Who wants to say, "My husband doesn't ever make love to me"? He was well respected and well liked. He had a real heart for encouragement. He remembered names and cared about people—a real people person.

He soon told me he was spiraling downward with his "habit." I didn't know how serious it was.

I never saw him masturbate. Along with the porn, it was his secret activity. I finally said, "I know what we're dealing with, Rick. You are passively abusing me. You haven't said very mean things to me and you're not physically abusive to me. But you are passively abusing me through this." He hung his head and agreed. That was a week before he died.

A few months earlier he had gained a lot of weight, developed a sudden and acute acne problem, and was diagnosed with a blood clot in his leg. He wondered what God was saying, and I told him God was giving warning. He said he was "clean before the Lord." He was in such denial that he really believed it. I found out later that during those months, he was having an affair. The woman actually visited him often when he spent a week in the hospital for his blood clot. I had no idea but found out the weekend Rick died.

The woman went to our pastor and confessed it. Apparently, all along, he had made a vow to her that if she told anyone about the affair, he would kill himself. She finally caved to the pressure and could no longer bear that burden. She went to the pastor. She was a Christian woman, one of my friends. It's important for us to know that we're not in some kind of bubble just because we're in the pew. Satan roams in many places.

I learned of the affair the day before Rick died. In the same twenty-four-hour period of time I learned of the affair, confronted Rick in a meeting with our pastor, and received word that he had committed suicide.

On that Sunday, the pastor called Rick in right before the evening service and told him he knew everything and was coming to our house after church. At that service, a woman got up and said, "I don't know who this is for, but God says, 'I am a Father to the fatherless and husband to the widow.'" I remembered that the next morning—and *every* day since Rick has been gone. Rick was resolved to kill himself. He was overcome by darkness.

We got home from Sunday night service and were hardly even in the door and you can imagine what had to take place—changing the clothes of all seven children, getting them into bed, tucking them in. And before we even started the rituals, Rick told me the pastor was on his way over.

"He's coming over *here* tonight? You just had a meeting with him. Why is he coming over here?"

He answered in a dull tone, "Well, he's coming over here because he wants to tell you I had an affair. But I'm not supposed to tell you, he is." So here again was "I'm your best friend so let me tell you real quick; let me warn you what's going to happen." It was a bittersweet thing. I was so full of anger and so full of shock. I knew things were cool between us physically, but how could he ever walk this road again? I hated having to go through it. I was scared for him. I felt some level of comfort that the pastor would come alongside me this time. It was encouraging to know that someone would come over and care enough to tell us what to do. Someone else could be the bad guy and tell Rick this was not acceptable.

I really lost it. I was trying to put my children to bed and just lost it. I went out on the back porch with the same overwhelming feeling that I experienced the first time. It's almost an out-of-body thing: numbness, loss of breath, panic, rage. It was horrible.

The pastor came. Rick was only *physically* there; he just sat in a daze. I was determined that I would be very careful about what came out of my mouth. I was going to listen. The pastor was very encouraging, very positive. "We're going to walk through this together. You're going to make it. There's hope for your marriage." But Rick just sat there. There was no repentance; he just wasn't there.

At the end, the pastor finally said to him, "Well, do you have anything to say?"

Not looking at anybody, Rick said, "I'm very suicidal right this moment."

We kind of ended after that. The pastor left, and I remember I was really, really angry with Rick. Because he had played the "suicide card" so many times before, I never even considered taking him seriously this time. I felt like he was manipulating me and the pastor to get us to feel sorry for him. I was so mad.

In the troubled mind, suicide is the most selfless thing to do. They won't have to be a bother anymore, to ruin people's lives. That's what the Enemy tells them. They are not thinking clearly.

Rick would often say that I'd be better off without him

and that he was tired of hurting me. I believe he meant that, but if one person has said so to me, then it's been a hundred: "It was the most *selfish* thing he could've ever done."

Finally we went to bed at 4:30 in the morning. I only slept one hour that night. We tossed and turned for an hour and finally at 5:30, Rick got up and left. It never crossed my mind he was going to do it. He left and came back. I never asked him where he went. I was too mad. I was so furious, and I was exhausted after one hour of sleep. He came back, took a shower, and got ready to go to work, as if he had just woken up at 6:00. He got all the children up, fed them breakfast, and never said anything to me.

I know now he went to get all his supplies to carry out the suicide. He went to the bait and tackle store and then to a home supply store.

We went downstairs, and I asked him some questions about the affair that now I regret. He answered the questions and elaborated a little. Knowing the other woman and being friends with her made it so much worse.

Rick left for a doctor's appointment for his leg. He called me at 10:30 and told me he just wanted me to know he got a clean bill of health. Like nothing happened the night before! It was Jekyll and Hyde again. Before he hung up, he said, "Well, I just wanted to let you know I miss you." He never said, "I'm sorry, I love you," but just "I miss you." That was really weird to me. It was his way of saying good-bye. And that was to be our final conversation.

I went through the whole day and kept busy. I took the kids out for dinner, and we got ice cream and went to the park. Our pastor called me and he was wonderful. He said, "I've decided that as a church, we're going to care for you and see you and Rick through this. If you want to go off for a weekend, we'll pay for baby-sitting; we'll pay for a vacation for you. If you just need to buy something important, we'll cover it. We'll stand by you. We are all family." That was very encouraging. My heart was blessed.

I stayed out of the house all day and came home after dinner to get the kids washed and changed into pajamas. Two plainclothes Tulsa police officers came to the door and told me the most dreaded news. Rick had committed suicide. He had hanged himself. I stood quietly for several minutes. The officers got nervous. The older one asked, "Don't you want to scream? Don't you want to cry?"

"No, sir, but I need to make some calls, and I will wait for the body of Christ to surround me." That may have sounded strange, but I felt carried, lifted, somehow shielded. I didn't ask much about Rick's suicide. To this day, a lot of people know more details than I know. How would it help?

There was a huge funeral with a closed casket. I conducted most of the ceremony. The two pastors said they had never had the widow do the funeral before. I apologized and explained my strong leading. I knew I was the only one who could get up there and share with passion. I knew the big picture. I refused to have to sit back and pretend that Rick's suicide was a surprise to me. I *did* know why he took his own life. I did not share details, but I was able to share some truths and generalities. I was the only one who could get up there and speak forgiveness over the other woman, who was present. I was the only one who could get up there and speak blessing over my children. I knew I was to get up and give glory to God for the ways He carried us and provided over the years.

Talk about being in control. I was not in control anymore. For the next two years, I never bought groceries. The Lord let me know that groceries would come into the house. And they did. People shopped for me. They would bring groceries, I would try to pay them, and they wouldn't allow it. So not only were groceries delivered, they were paid for. It went on for two solid years. In a physical body, the antibodies come to the rescue for however long it takes. The body of Christ is a bandage over the wound until the Lord starts to bring a real healing. Some people don't need two years, but it took us two years to begin to operate with some normalcy. I couldn't even pick up the phone for two years.

And in some ways it has taken longer. We just marked the fifth year. It has been five years of grief, with all different shadings. The second year was the hardest. I realized on my way to meet you that today is my wedding anniversary. The Lord has been so good. You can become addicted to grief and find your significance in that. This is who I am. My significance was found in being a widow. That's just a reality.

I could choose at any moment to jump into bed, pull the covers over my head, and decide I'm going to be depressed. And the Enemy will dangle that in front of me when things get too overwhelming. I created a mentor board to help me parent the children, and I'm very real with my mentors. It's humbling, but I know I need accountability and I need a group of people that I can go to and say, "This is what I'm going through today. I'm not doing very well with these seven kids. It's a hard road.

FOR YOUR MAKER IS YOUR HUSBAND— THE LORD ALMIGHTY IS HIS NAME—THE HOLY ONE OF ISRAEL IS YOUR REDEEMER; HE IS CALLED THE GOD OF ALL THE EARTH.

—ISAIAH 54:5

There are times when I don't like it." Yes, it would be better if their father were here. Some things are harder, but in many ways I am more at peace not to have that emotional abuse. God is sovereign.

Reflections on Finding Joy in the Morning

For someone going through anything like this, my major advice would be, don't go numb spiritually. You can go numb every other way, but not spiritually. And I really heeded that counsel. I'm just the mom, just the vessel. I'm a vessel for these kids, I'm not their saving grace. I don't have to be supermom because they don't have a dad. You don't have to be everything to everyone. I just try to relax. I don't stay relaxed—I don't have a relaxed temperament— but I do know God is handling things, and He's going to take care of whatever comes our way. My favorite verse is 2 Corinthians 4:15 (NKJV): "All things are for your sakes, that grace, having spread through the many, may cause thanks- giving to abound to the glory of God." God is in the midst of all this, and He is going to let us make His name known and people will come to the Lord because of all this. And it's a conscious surrender every single day to just be the mom. I *don't* have to be or do everything.

I almost laugh when I hear people say, "She's in the anger stage right now." I think sarcastically, *Oh, that's pretty neat. How long does it last? I'm so looking forward to the next stage. What's that next stage?*

People want to neatly categorize pain and grief. I found myself reading books that categorized it. If I slipped back into a denial stage, I was just going to pretend that Rick was going to come home that night. The anger is surely an emotion that does come and go. And I think that's why "seventy times seven" is required when we forgive. I would love to have packed the anger and forgiveness in a little box and put it on the shelf and said, "Good riddance—that's over!" It was kind of surprising when I found out it wasn't.

My oldest daughter just got her driver's license, and she's out there doing her parallel parking. And a surprising thing happened; I found myself wanting to call Rick. "You ought to see her, honey, she's parallel parking. I think she's going to fail the test because she's not doing very well, but you'd be proud anyway." I was desperately wanting my husband, which was a feeling I hadn't felt in while. I knew he would've been there cheering her on. And I found myself really, really angry that he wasn't there. He chose this. All this anger was a surprise attack.

On the way home I asked my daughter, "How do you feel?"

"Good, Mom. But I kind of missed Daddy being there."

We had never talked at length about her dad's death, and I said, "Aren't you kind of mad?"

But the kids won't go there with me; they won't go to the "mad." Sometimes I have to say, "Well, *I'm* mad, and you ought to be mad, because if he hadn't killed himself he would've been here for us!" Then, I eventually come around; the Lord is faithful.

I said to my daughter, "Don't you wish we could have at least called him to tell him we're on the way home and that you *did* get your driver's license?"

It's the markers and milestones that hurt the most. At her eighth-grade graduation, I sat and cried through the whole thing. That was three years after Rick died, and it was so surprising to me. And I know now—the proms, the graduations, the weddings, and the grandchildren—I'll be marking those milestones without him.

After my daughter passed her test, the Lord prompted her driver's instructor to call that day and ask, "Did you get your license? You did? I'm so proud of you!"

✠

Yes, I've forgiven him and yes, it's ongoing. I'm mad he never got free of the addiction and yet glad he's released from the pain. I really loved him. The Lord often searches me. I still hate the fact that Rick killed himself, and we're having to deal with that complexity. I wonder, *Why couldn't it have been the blood clot, God? Why didn't he die from that? That would've been more natural, easier for us to bear.*

From what I hear, many young people think about suicide, and this adds to the odds of them taking that step. It is not a natural thing to kill yourself. It's a very supernatural thing in a negative sense. That's what I tell my kids. I'll say, "If the Enemy is going to come around and try to give you similar thoughts that he gave your daddy, just know that it's not natural, not healthy, not God's plan for you. Daddy was confused and feeling lost and in deep pain. Satan comes to kill, steal, and destroy. Daddy really believed those thoughts, that those bad plans were for him."

✠

Suicide. It's so devastating. I would encourage anyone who's dealing with the suicide of a loved one to try not to keep asking the same questions. I have to keep remembering that myself. You have to come to a point where you just don't look back—kind of the opposite of Lot's wife who *did* look back. You just have to come to the point where you realize that you cannot do anything more about it. No more looking back to the dreaded event—only to the sweet memories. That said, you do have to embrace the pain for a season. It's okay for it to hurt. Grief is like childbirth. If you want something good to happen here you're going to have to hurt for a little. Trust that it's going to be much better in a while. Get excited for what God is about to do—expect a miracle.

Blame is futile and will make you sick. In one book I read on grief, it said you bring everyone into the "courtroom" of your own heart. In my case it's the pastor, the neighbors, the friends, the adversaries, the other woman, myself, circumstances—and I try to place blame. Shouldn't I have taken his threats to hurt himself more seriously? Couldn't the pastor have handled things differently? Didn't any friend care enough to check in with him more? There's *got* to be somebody to blame for this! It's worthy of blame! We must all surrender that blame game and rest in the fact that God is sovereign. No one is sentenced in the courtroom of grief. You give up your right to be the judge.

God is even on the stand at one point. We may rail at God, saying, "God, *You* are to blame. You are the sovereign God, and You could have stopped it! I prayed for You to stop it. We both saw it coming, God." It was a huge thing for me to realize I was mad at God, because good Christian girls aren't mad at God. And finally I realized I thought He was mad at me because He'd have to be mad at me considering all I've been through. I must have done something really bad to deserve my husband killing himself. It's all back to being my fault. It took a while to realize that God's not mad at me and I don't need to be mad at God. I trust His sovereignty.

> **The Lord will guide you always; he will satisfy your needs in a sun-scorched land and will strengthen your frame. You will be like a well-watered garden, like a spring whose waters never fail.**
>
> **—Isaiah 58:11**

My kids are great, and they're doing well. They really are doing okay. The mentor board has been a huge blessing. There are seven couples and they've provided wisdom and counsel. When I knew my first child was going to be a teenager, I kind of got cold feet. They've stepped up to the plate with advice and a lot of practical support. They are involved with the kids' lives. Their commitment is to one child for a year at a time, so no one is overwhelmed.

If you're hurting, just know you're going to be okay because God is faithful. God is good no matter what our perception of good is. This doesn't feel good. It didn't feel good when Rick was out of control, but I still had to believe that God is good, despite my circumstances. I have really trusted Him and walked in that. He is a good God. The pain? The ache? It doesn't make sense. It never will.

The grief begins to fade. It gets easier. Joy comes in the morning.

The joy of the Lord is my strength. I am empowered by the joy of the Lord. The Lord really keeps assuring me, "You don't know exactly where you're going, but I will be with you every step of the way. I've got a plan in all of this; just trust Me." He assures me that He chose me to be His child. I didn't always feel chosen by my husband.

I am healing. The Lord really does do things to make me feel that this didn't catch Him by surprise. My significance is no longer in being a widow, but for now I really love the adventure of having God being my husband and the kids' father. Peace will come to those who put their trust and hope in God.

In this crazy world, there's an enormous distinction between good times and bad, between sorrow and joy.... But in the eyes of God, they're never separated. Where there is pain, there is healing; where there is mourning, there is dancing; where there is poverty, there is the kingdom.

—Henri Nouwen

CHAPTER SEVEN

Catherine: Living through Loss, Embracing Eternity

Catherine's story is about lots of things: life and death, hope and despair, motherhood and miracles.

We met at her elegant home in a suburb of Phoenix. Catherine is articulate, graceful, and comfortable with her lavish surroundings. She and her husband were married five years ago, and she quickly described him as a wonderful man. That's probably because, since there was no food in the house, he happily served himself a chips-and-salsa dinner before disappearing upstairs to his study for the evening. (My kind of guy.)

Brian is forty-seven and Catherine is thirty-seven. A sophisticated blonde, she smiled with a knowing wink and told me she wanted someone older, wiser, and more experienced in the world. They are professional consultants and preside over their own company.

IN HER OWN WORDS: CATHERINE'S STORY

We felt very blessed to find each other. I was thirty-two when we married. For me, it was not late in life, but everyone said it should've happened sooner. We met on a blind date and instantly knew. I had basically sworn off men and even bought some fine furniture and four elegant place settings because I didn't want to wait for a man in order to have nice things.

Because we were ten years older than most newlyweds, we didn't want to let a lot of time go by before we married. I felt the Lord had given us both a quiet assurance that we were right for one another. We had a wonderful courtship and soon after the wedding, we agreed that trying to conceive was the next step. It was natural for us to discuss having children right away.

Obviously, there was a lot of pressure from parents, especially my parents. It's cultural. I also think, generally with women, whether they are strangers or somebody you haven't seen in a while, the conversation always leads to "Are you pregnant? Do you have children? Do you plan to have a family?" It always comes back to that. But in those first six months of marriage I had not gotten pregnant, and I knew there could be something wrong.

I know a fertility specialist, so I didn't have any hesitation; I met with him immediately to see what was going on so we could create a plan of attack. Then we got started on it.

Basically, when you start fertility treatments you have to rule out what is causing you not to become pregnant. So they do a series of four different tests, three of which are directed toward the woman. Obviously, there have been an increasing number of men who have some problem, so now they test the man. They ruled out anything alarming in our case.

They were able to figure out that my tubes were just too small. It was simple biological anatomy. Nothing could get through the tubes; therefore, I could not conceive. They said in vitro fertilization (IVF) would be the best option for us. Our doctor said we could try other things, but due to our age and comfortable finances we were placed on a fast track, and we opted to move directly to IVF.

It was my egg and his sperm, and I conceived. It was really great—and unusual. Usually in vitro couples don't conceive on the first try. We certainly were surprised. "Oh, my gosh, it works!" It was scary. I was never the type of little girl nor did I become a young woman whose goal it was to have babies. Babies were kind of intimidating, but I was delighted and excited.

I grew and had regular visits to the specialist. That first pregnancy was a little unusual because I didn't know what to expect. I didn't know what I didn't know. When you are pregnant through an infertility doctor, they monitor you fairly closely. They were monitoring a lot of different things, but there is no mystery about when you conceived, and they work from that date on. So they lined up all these dates that I had to come back in. One appointment was to hear the fetal heartbeat. Going through IVF, they sometimes put more fertilized eggs into you, so you could possibly have multiple pregnancies. So I went in to hear the fetal heartbeat and to find out whether there was one heartbeat or two.

My mom went with me, and she was so excited because it would be her first grandbaby. I knew nothing; I just took her because I thought, *Well, I've got to take someone,* and Brian wasn't available. We went in there, and the doctor's face said it all. There was absolutely no heartbeat. I had no symptoms of a miscarriage. I probably wouldn't have even known what the signs were. He just said there was no heartbeat. I don't think he was able to do a miscarriage procedure, so I had to come back later for a dilation and curettage (D&C). It was the eleventh week, almost the first full term of trimester.

That was really hard—especially after the D&C procedure. I didn't have a lot of girlfriends who had been pregnant, and

I was not very experienced with the whole pregnancy thing, so I had told everyone the very first day I knew I was pregnant. I announced, "I am pregnant! Yea!" I didn't know about waiting until the first trimester to be over. I was ignorant.

The downside of what I did, telling everyone I was pregnant, was I had to confront that issue over and over and over. It was very hard to connect with people on an emotional and spiritual level when I shared I had a miscarriage. What I found was that people didn't know what to say. They obviously didn't know how to respond. "It's okay—you'll have more children." The responses were almost as painful as losing the baby because they often negated the whole experience.

Then I started doing a lot of reading. In a magazine at my doctor's office I read a story about how they handle miscarriage in Japan. The whole village of women comes around and helps; they mourn and create a memorial for miscarried babies. They have this big cemetery full of small markers of babies that have been miscarried! I thought, *How amazing that if we really believe that this is a life, then it is really a death, and it needs to be treated as such. It needs response. Sympathy cards need to be sent, or notes, or just encouragement and acknowledgment that even though you didn't meet that child, there was a love and a bond there that started instantaneously.*

What you need is someone to acknowledge that child's life and that child's death and your loss—to help you have some sense of closure. Even the word *miscarriage* doesn't necessarily apply. My baby's heartbeat just stopped. I didn't expel the child, but I would say, "I had a miscarriage." I didn't know what else to say.

There were so many things that should *not* have been said. I should have written them down because they were very hurtful at the time: "You can always have more children"; "Don't worry about it, you'll get pregnant again";

"God knows what He's doing." Most people in my case did not know that we had already spent a lot of time and money to try to conceive this child. But you don't really want to get into that with people. It is not an easy road when you start down it, trying to get pregnant and not being successful. Then you try again, and you feel God is still calling you. You think, *He is not closing the door. He is just making it a little more challenging. He wants to see if we're going to persevere and have faith.*

Each individual couple needs to make their own decision on what road to go down if they can't conceive naturally, whether it's choosing to go to the medical community or adoption or surrogate pregnancy. There are lots of options. There is a tremendous group of aging women trying to have children. When you say, "Oh, you can have other children," that can be insensitive because nobody realizes how far you have come just to even get there. But I also try not to dwell on hurts. I try to remember all the good things people said.

I believe no one intentionally set out to hurt me. Those people who I thought were doing it out of ignorance, I confronted in love. I just said, "This is not helpful at this time." I am not shy about doing that because I knew that is what I needed to be able to do to keep friendships and family relationships intact.

I truly grieved. The hardest part for me was losing a dream. You start down this path, and you have all these visions as any expectant mom would have, and you just think of all these amazing things. You think of the nine months, and then you think about what they will look like. You start down this whole road of planning—whether it's right or wrong, unfortunately, that is the way women are wired. But the hardest part for me that sad day was seeing the look on my doctor's face, who was a dear friend, and my mom's, who was to be a grandma, and having to come home and tell my husband—to see the pain they had to go through. I think the grief process for me started there. I had not really had a chance to bond on a very deep emotional level with that tiny life. I looked at other's dreams being crushed, and then I started thinking about my own. I said, "Of course! This is a life and it is gone!" Then the reality set in and it became very difficult.

NOW FAITH IS BEING SURE OF WHAT WE HOPE FOR AND CERTAIN OF WHAT WE DO NOT SEE.

—HEBREWS 11:1

I wasn't sure how I was supposed to feel, but I think it set me back in my faith. "Lord, was this the right course of action, or did we jump the gun? Did we do something maybe we shouldn't have? Are You trying to steer us toward adoption?" My husband and I were not set on having our own children, but when we were told there was no medical reason why we couldn't, we just felt IVF was the option we wanted to pursue.

Once you go through something, you look back and say, "What could I have done differently? Did we make the right decisions? Did we properly analyze it? Did we spend enough time on our knees praying? Did we spend enough time talking as a couple? Talking with the doctors to make the right decisions?" It's easy to obsess.

I threw myself into God's arms and the arms of very

capable medical professionals. I totally trusted in the Lord. I knew He had plans. I didn't know how it was going to end, and that's just how I started the healing. I went on this wave and I was just going along. There were some hard days. Maybe I could have done something to change the outcome. Then I started reading too much about pregnancy, and I started thinking, *What did I do?* There are so many dos and don'ts that can confuse a first-time mom. There are some people who say, "You can't eat this; you can't exercise." There were two or three people who said things like, "You shouldn't have been working at one of your client's houses because you were going up and down the steps. And you were working too hard. Your activity may have caused the miscarriage." That was hard. But the infertility specialist assured me, "You had absolutely zilch to do with this. Unfortunately, the fertilized egg was not strong enough." God allowed this life to end. It wasn't anything I did or didn't do. Maybe back in our grandparents' day, there were lots of theories. Now, there is so much information—sometimes it's too much to absorb.

In the months that followed, I didn't really withdraw or anything like that. I pretty much stayed the same. When I embarked on the "infertility road," it was tough anyway. It was not something that I was embarrassed about. I was very open with my family and my friends. I told everybody what I was doing. I didn't even know that it was a controversial subject that caused division. People have strong feelings about IVF. Maybe I lived my life too openly. Once I told women I was doing this, many confided that they had done it. Many had tried for five to ten years and were not success-ful, and they had never shared it with anyone. So I found myself connecting with a lot of new people and very strangely so. I found myself trying to help people who had already gone through it but who had inner conflict about it.

It was a different group of women than my close friends. My family was always very much a part of this. They were told every detail whether they wanted to hear it or not! I just didn't know any better. I didn't know that some things should be kept private.

Unless you understand IVF and unless you really are comfortable with it, it is definitely unusual. It is not "natural." It is not the way that most people feel that pregnancy should happen.

In vitro fertilization is when they give a woman a series of shots for three to four weeks to help regulate her follicles to do their jobs, and then the eggs will mature. Then they remove the egg and join it with the husband's sperm in a Petri dish. It fertilizes for three days. Then they put that fertilized embryo back into the woman, hoping it will be accepted in the uterus. They bypass the fallopian tubes and all of the areas that typically cause women to have trouble.

So IVF is a very valuable option; it is an amazing process. There are so many healthy, beautiful in vitro babies. They called them "test tube" babies back in the old days. But the process for the woman is very challenging.

I think the shots themselves, which I had to give to myself, were *more* than challenging. I was a girly girl, and not having had children, I had never before had to care for cuts on the knees or bloody elbows or anything like that. So when they told me I was going to have give myself shots, not once but twice a day, I said, "Are you crazy? I can't do that." Then they had me practice on an orange. I told my husband that was the hardest part of the whole process. I lost my trust in God for a while.

My body gets agitated with just the thought of needles. When I faced having to do this to myself, I really crumbled, and I was getting a little upset with God. I said, "I really can't believe I have to do this, but this is the course set out for me, though I hate needles." To some people that part is not a big deal, but to me that was a huge deal. I gave myself shots twice a day for three weeks. The first time I did it we were traveling. I will never forget it. I sat for forty-five minutes because I just couldn't do it. I did everything they told me to do. I was sterilized. I was ready to go. I had mixed the drugs just so. (That was another thing I had to cope with. I am not very good with numbers or millimeters, so I was afraid I was going to give myself too much or too little.) I sat there, and I could not inflict that pain on myself! It felt so unnatural. But I tried to stop and pray, to think of the bigger picture, that I was doing this for something much greater than myself. I think that's when God started showing me what motherhood would be: sacrificing my own needs, my own feelings, and my own comfort for somebody else—or even for the *idea* (in my case) of somebody else. I did it, and some days were harder than others. Some days I was so proud of myself I would call to Brian, "I did it without any hesitation!" I was just so proud of how far I had come in being able to get through that physical and emotional challenge.

I didn't have anybody in my life who ever negated our choice to pursue in vitro. To me, that mentality would be the same as those who refuse to get medical treatment or take a blood transfusion. There are people who fall into this because of religious convictions. If you had cancer, you could choose to let God heal you or you could look into ways that modern science could participate in your healing. We had prayed about it, and we knew we were going to look into— and hopefully benefit from—this "miraculous" option.

We each had a big decision to make: "Do I take six months to a year and mourn or grieve, or do I just keep moving forward with this?" We sought spiritual and medical counsel and we prayed about it. We made the decision to try it again after the allotted time—three months. So we had the miscarriage in November, and started another round of in vitro in January.

Beginning Again with a Hopeful Heart

The second time we were a little gun shy, a little fearful, and a little bit more prepared. There was not the same excitement, yet we had a quiet resolve that we were going to continue to see this through, no matter what. We reminded ourselves that we sat at our dining room table a year earlier and gave it all to the Lord, not knowing what the outcome was going to be, just starting to understand for the first time in practical terms what faith must be. Faith has to be a quiet, confident assurance that God is going to do what is right for you, even though you may not understand it, you may not appreciate it, you may not want it at the time. I had heard that my entire life, but I don't think I ever really put it into practice until then. I had to believe and to know that He is a loving God, that the ultimate outcome of infertility treatments, whether we get pregnant or not, is not an indicator of His love for us. He was just calling us to be obedient to what we were sensing as a couple.

So we tried it again, and, lo and behold, we got that phone call, and we were pregnant again! Another miracle. I remember getting that call. I was upstairs in the bedroom because once you do all the procedures you have to kind of take it easy for a few days to make sure everything goes well. I was lying low, and my husband was outside doing something, so I yelled out the window, "We're pregnant!" The excitement was right back. I mean, it does all happen again, and as any mother knows, unless it is an unwanted pregnancy, there is an excitement you cannot contain. It is immediate. All of a sudden this life is living inside you. With IVF, you know sooner rather than later. It was really wonderful.

This time, though, I told no one—only my husband and my mother because they were the two who meant the most to me. They shared the deepest pain the last time. I knew I couldn't contain it, number one, but I also needed their support as well. Weeks later, I did tell an immediate circle of friends and family who I felt would continue to pray for us, lift our pregnancy up, and be joyful with us, but who would also be there in case something didn't go right. So we took it slowly, one day at a time. That is when I learned the meaning of "one day at a time."

I had some complications early on. I started bleeding heavily and thought this was a real miscarriage, versus what had happened to me before. We went into the doctor's office and they examined me and the baby. There was a heartbeat, but the sonogram showed two sacks. Their best guess was that I had conceived twins and that one of the twins had not made it. The fact that there was still a heartbeat was encouraging, but there was also sadness, to think, *Oh, no, this is happening all over again.*

Our minds can be so wonderful as far as selective memory, but at the same time they certainly can jolt you right back to where you were when something negative happens. I was reliving it all again. I got scared and afraid of the future. Self-doubt came in: "Should we have done this?" "Did we do it too soon?" We had all of those doubts. Then

I AM THE LORD, YOUR GOD, WHO TAKES HOLD OF YOUR RIGHT HAND AND SAYS TO YOU, DO NOT FEAR; I WILL HELP YOU.

—ISAIAH 41:13

you take a deep breath and realize that God is still in control. He was sovereign the last go-around even before we were pregnant, even before we were married. He is still the same God. He has not changed. These circumstances are changing, and Satan would love for fear and doubt to enter in. I felt a spiritual battle, but I was prepared. It was a choice that I had to make. I am going to continue to trust God and the faith that I have found, or I am going to choose fear.

> **WE DO NOT WANT YOU TO BECOME LAZY, BUT TO IMITATE THOSE WHO THROUGH FAITH AND PATIENCE INHERIT WHAT HAS BEEN PROMISED.**
>
> **—HEBREWS 6:12**

When I recommitted my life to Jesus as an adult, I didn't know the road in front of me. Up until then, I had no major struggles or challenges or anything that would make me question my faith. *Why do I believe what I believe? And do I really believe it? And can I put it in practice even after tragedy strikes?* Now, my very foundation was being tested.

I think it goes back to faith. Do you really have faith, or do you not? Satan was attacking me *and* my faith. *Am I really going to trust God?* I had already committed to do just that. I had already said, "I will trust Him no matter what." I started a journal and I think the first page was, "I am trusting You no matter what...." There were no other words. I couldn't even begin to tell God what I wanted. I wanted a healthy baby just as any mother wants. I didn't care whether it was a boy or a girl. I didn't care if it had ten fingers and ten toes. At that point in time I just wanted my baby to be healthy. I was going to do everything in my power to help give this baby a good environment. Other than that, I knew it was in God's hands. I didn't think I could control the baby's life or death, but I knew that I could contribute to the environment. I could eat right, get rest, and stay off my feet if that is what they were telling me to do.

The doctor put me on bed rest. It is so difficult for a "type A" person to be flat on her back or lying on her left side, which is how they preferred me to be. All these modern instruments give them a snapshot, but they don't know exactly what's going on. Patience is developed one day at a time—one day at a time.

After about eleven weeks (the same week I lost the first baby), we realized that the second baby was growing and things were going well. I had a few good weeks where they let me get up, and I was doing normal things. I took on a client or two, and I did some things around the house. Then, unfortunately, I started bleeding heavily once again. In my mind, I immediately thought *that was it. We tried, but it's over. Three strikes and you're out. This was it. This was my third loss.* I drove like a crazed lunatic down to the doctor's office to check the heartbeat. Brian went with me. I could not imagine going through what I have been through without having a loving spouse.

Again, the baby was fine. So *why* was I bleeding? Why was I cramping? No answers, no answers whatsoever. It was very frustrating—especially for my husband. Guys want concrete answers. At that time I was more willing to accept vagueness. We would get through another few days, and I would have good days, then, boom, I would start bleeding again. So it was back and forth, back and forth—I can't tell you how many times. I got my Day-timer and started keeping track—heavy bleeding, light bleeding, heavy cramping, mild cramping—just so I would be better able to tell the doctors, because they got to the point where they said, "Look, you can't come in here every time." So I learned to live with it. I learned to live with the fear that every day I could be losing this child. I was transferred to a high-risk OB/GYN practice and found that the level of care was much more what I needed at the time. They monitored the baby a little more frequently, and I didn't drop everything every time I bled. I got to a comfort level there. So we just ended up taking it one day at a time. I had three to four months of heavy bleeding.

IN HIM OUR HEARTS REJOICE, FOR WE TRUST IN HIS HOLY NAME.

—PSALM 33:21

On a personal, somewhat comical side note, I was so excited not to have to get my period when I got pregnant, and then I bled throughout the whole pregnancy! Oh, well.

I stayed on bed rest. I had girlfriends come visit. I had family stop by. My husband took good care of me. I was thankful that he was able to work from home at the time. I tried not to disturb him. I tried to give him the day so he felt like he was at work. I read on a bed-rest Web site that you should set up your room so you're not too dependent on people. I would have a pitcher of water, my laptop, my telephone numbers, everything I needed up there all on the side table. We tried to make the best of it. I read a lot of books. I thought a lot. I made the mistake of watching the Discovery Channel on healthy pregnancies or child growth or whatever, and I just boo-hooed every time. I watched a lot of home improvement shows. If I was really feeling down, I would turn to one of those talk shows and see how awful other peoples' lives were to conclude mine was okay!

After five months, the specialist started to realize that my baby, a girl, was not growing. They couldn't figure out why I was still bleeding so heavily. It was June 2003. They were trying not to worry me, but I would rather know what I am dealing with. I am not good with generalities. I like specifics. We used to commit to praying that our baby would grow just a little bit. We would keep track of how much she grew. We would praise God, and we would thank Him when she grew. I took great joy in the little things.

I said, "If I am going to have this experience only one time, I am going to enjoy it. I don't know if I will be pregnant ever again. I don't want to be so caught up in all the 'what ifs' and not enjoy this experience." So I kept looking forward to the day that I would feel her kick or move. That day never came. I once felt a very minor flutter on July fourth. I got permission to sit in the swimming pool. I had nothing much to show—a little kangaroo pouch—and didn't even look pregnant. I was lying on a float, and—I will never forget—something moved! I saw it, and it was the most amazing experience. It was so tiny, you wouldn't even know what part of the body it was because it was so small. It could have been her head, I don't know. But that was just so exciting. Those little things kept me going.

I thought, *I don't care what the doctors are saying; I just know that every verse about hope and life in my Bible is underlined.* "He formed me in the womb." It says that in the Bible. I don't have to worry. My doctor didn't form her. I didn't form her. God formed her. Maybe it was in a Petri dish, but that embryo had to implant in *my* uterus and grow. He formed that child. He knew her. He knew every hair on her head, and I believed that with all my heart, even when she was small and not growing. So I just took it one day at a time.

The lessons I had started to learn as I was dealing with my miscarriages were all being reinforced—one day at a time. I had to trust one day at a time. Sometimes I just needed to get through the next hour. I now understand what some addiction programs teach about just getting through that next hour.

My view of what made for "a great day" drastically changed.

The next visit to the doctor was fairly sad because he said the baby had not grown much. He said we would probably have to make arrangements to take her out early to put her in a better "environment." He was referring to the Neonatal Intensive Care Unit (NICU). The modern technology they had would help her grow better than my environment. Something was preventing her from growing. At this point in time they still had no answers. It was the first week in August. They were probably the darkest days of my life to that point. My husband was on a business trip. As usual, the cramps came, the blood, the whole nine yards, but at three o'clock in the morning, I just felt weird, an incredible pressure. And I thought, *Oh, no! The baby is going to come out.* I tried to reach my husband.

I got into the bathroom and I passed a clot ten inches in diameter—I mean huge! I didn't know it was a blood clot at the time; I thought it was the placenta. I was thinking, *Okay, this is it! The baby is next!* I didn't *realize* that normally the baby comes out first and then the afterbirth. Ignorance is bliss in my case. I got super angry with God that He allowed this to happen the *one* night that my husband wasn't there. I called my doctor, and he said, "There's nothing we can do if you're losing this baby. Wait until nine o'clock and come in. You can go to the emergency room and wait, but there is nothing they can do."

I was in week twenty-eight. I had been told a week earlier that if our baby was born within the next four weeks, she might not survive. They were telling me I had to get to thirty-two weeks—maybe thirty at the extreme minimum. They said the baby would not survive if she was delivered sooner.

Two days later, I was in the hospital, and the doctor told me the baby wouldn't survive. She was way too small. We were at twenty-eight weeks, which in a normal, healthy pregnancy would have very good chances of survival. I was told I would be moved to the larger hospital in the city. The choice was to stay where I was and have the baby stillborn, or to go downtown and deliver her. Those were my choices.

So I had to lose the doctor I had been seeing as well as any comfort level. Night was falling. We were going to lose her. We all came this far; we did everything we could, and we were going to lose her. It was just overwhelming. We were at the point of no return. You just go forward. I have a lot of admiration now for people who are firefighters or military personnel or doctors who are making life-and-death decisions. You get to a point in time where you just *have* to move forward. You *have* to trust. You are going into that fire, not knowing if you are going to come out. You *have* to do it. I really felt I had to go forward. I had to give this child a chance. I had to trust that God was moving me to the right place. He was intervening at the right time. He was surrounding me with angels.

The attending doctor said, "I will give her every chance, but I'm going to tell you—she is not going to make it. I am so sorry you had to be transferred here to have this news given to you." I looked at her and I said, "I have to trust God. He's gotten me this far." My faith became so real. I needed to say to the doctor, "Look, I'm not going to hold you responsible for one thing that goes wrong or right in that room. I appreciate the fact that you have monitored me, that you have monitored my baby, and that you have cared for us. You're trying your best to make right decisions. We're going to pray as a family. I'm going to pray as a mother. If you would like to stay here and join us as a doctor, that's fine." She stayed.

I thought, *Lord, if I am here to witness to this doctor, this is going to be really hard because right now I want to be a mom. I don't want to be a Christian. I want to be a mom! I don't want to be sharing my faith. I want my baby!*

We proceeded to the delivery room. Our daughter was fifteen ounces and a little less than nine inches. When they made the incision, she squirmed up into my rib cage. The doctor didn't want to hurt or damage her, so she made the decision to do a "T" incision, once the skin was pulled up over the flap. When she got the baby, she had to move my colon or intestines over, and apparently it infected my blood stream with E. coli. So once they got me stitched up, I immediately got a 104-degree temperature. It was just awful—everything went wrong. They took her away. She wasn't crying because she was not yet able; her lungs were too small. I sobbed.

She was born August 7 at 1:20 in the afternoon by emergency C-section, much to my dismay. When I was told she weighed fifteen ounces, I was still under sedation and I said, "Well, can you calculate that into pounds for me?"

"No, no, no—she isn't even a pound!" replied the nurse.

"What do mean she isn't even a pound? I gained twenty-two pounds with this pregnancy. What do you mean, she isn't even a pound?" I couldn't understand that she could be that small. How would I send out a birth announcement that says fifteen ounces? People are going to think it's a typo and that we left off the pounds!

I was introduced to the NICU staff. That was a whole new group of specialists trying to help our baby survive. My head was spinning. I was so tired. I was just exhausted. They only allowed me to see my daughter once. She was on the table. Once they realized I was getting a fever—from the E. coli—I could not see her for the first five days. I remember being wheeled in there to see her through the glass. I just could not believe it. She looked like a little frog. She had long limbs taped down to the tiny mattress in the incubator. Her legs were long and her arms were long, but her little body was so short, and her head was so big. Her eyes were still fused shut. I said, "She looks like a little frog!" I didn't know whether to be joyful or to cry. I looked at her for a long while and made an additional observation: "She's beautiful!" She was three months premature—we went from taking one day at a time to one minute at a time.

The baby had what was called "intrauterine growth restriction," which prevented her from growing. She measured more like a twenty-one- or twenty-three-week-old baby. She didn't connect to the placenta properly, and all the blood that should have been feeding her the nutrients was instead coming out of me. So she was deprived of oxygen and blood during the whole pregnancy. It was awful—for both of us. The things she had to endure; it hurts me as a mother to think about it. But God had her in the palm of His hand. I believe she didn't feel pain. I believe He had her mission planned and that was all part of it. Her story will impact people in ways we'll never know until heaven.

A Surprising Turn, a Show of Strength
She proved us all wrong. She made it through her first day! We were grateful, and the doctors were astounded. She lasted a day, and then she lasted another day and another day.

People had labored for days to save this child. They went through the ups and downs. Our prayer circle was so close that once she actually came into the world, they all felt instantly connected to her. And they were sending out APBs all over the world: *Pray for this little baby! Pray for her. Pray for this little child!*

The flowers, the cards, the letters and e-mails—it was just overwhelming. I couldn't help but think how she was touching so many lives.

People couldn't come by and visit because of the NICU restrictions. The whole pregnancy wasn't normal, the delivery wasn't normal, and now the visitation wasn't normal. She was fighting for her life. You can't take everyone in and say, "Here she is!" We tried to make the best of it one day at a time, and once I got over my illness, I decided in my heart and mind that no matter how many days or how many hours the Lord was going to give me with this child, I was going to enjoy every last one of them.

I decided I was going to stare at that little frog for as long as I could. If this were to be my only day with her, why would I want to be in a room by myself crying? I wanted to be looking at her! I wanted to be with her. I wanted to see her. I wanted to learn all I could about her in whatever time God gave me. It was a daily choice. Our daughter kept growing and surprising all the doctors, including the head honchos. I knew she was on her own course. I became a spectator—her most devoted fan.

I was very frustrated about not being able to hold and bond with my premature baby. I wanted all the stuff everybody tells you is so important. I was wondering, *How is she going to breast-feed? I can't even hold her!*

We were told we needed to make some decisions. "Do you or do you not wish to give a resuscitate order? Do you wish to hold your baby during and after death?" There are lots of technical, medical things that occur. I had no clue how it was going to end, but I would just hold on to all the prayers. There were prayer warriors who surrounded us, laboring in prayer for my daughter. So we watched her go from day to night to two months, to three months, to four months, to five months. Finally at five months they said, "You had better get the nursery ready. She is going to be coming home at the end of February."

We celebrated Alexa's first Christmas in the hospital. (Yes, we named her Alexa Faith). We celebrated Premature Awareness Day there. All the babies got a little stuffed animal from their friend Alexa. Five months passed with almost daily commutes to the hospital.

And we did try to live every day to the fullest. There were days and hours and minutes when we were told she just was not going to make it. We would go and pray, or we would go and cry. Or we would just go and hold each other. There were milestones, very beautiful milestones like being able to hold her the first time. I was giggling. I couldn't stop giggling because she was *so* little! She had a breathing tube inserted and I was afraid I would knock it out.

These babies are so strong. When my husband went in the very first time, Alexa knew her dad. She grabbed his finger and didn't let go. The first time her eyes opened—it was amazing. I slowly got involved with the other parents, but then I had some angels come and minister to me, too.

About the beginning of February, we were going into Alexa's sixth month. She started taking things by mouth. She breast-fed. She was doing well and was up to eight pounds. She had overcome so many issues. We were getting our house prepared to be able to handle oxygen and such. I had not gotten the room ready yet, so we took a few days off and decorated her nursery.

I went back in on Valentine's Day weekend. We were told she hadn't had a good night. I hadn't heard those words in two months. Our hearts sank. You can call NICU 24/7, so we called every night before we went to bed. She had been okay the night before, but that morning, they

said, "She didn't have a good night. Her oxygen require-
ment had gone up, so we have had to do some things that
we really didn't want to have to do." And then all of a sudden, it started all over, but this time I knew. I knew it was
over. It was the hardest thing to accept that her time here
was done.

My mother—a pillar of faith, an amazing woman of
God—just said, "She is going to overcome this." She
remained very positive.

I remember saying, "No." I don't know if it was because
I was so tired, or if it was God just letting me know. I definitely knew.

The doctor and nurses didn't say the words "She is
dying." Instead, they told us, "She didn't have a good night.
She's struggling. There are several options. We are going to
do whatever we can."

I pulled my stunned husband aside and said, "Brian, the
Lord has brought us this far with all these people. They've
watched us intimately for six whole months. They've watched
us from the time I arrived here in an ambulance to now. We
are not going to let our faith evaporate. They need to see it
now or never. They need to see us trusting God now more
than ever, even if it is not the outcome that we all want."

That's when it became super real. It was a conscious decision I made that we were going to go out with our faith
intact, not cursing God, not blaming God, and certainly not
viewing death as the end. That was important to me, and I
told my husband it was. I told him it was important to me
that even if it was my defense mechanism, I didn't care. Our
daughter had done her part—fought her fight. She lived six
months. She defied all odds. She had miracle after miracle
after miracle. I don't know why the Lord chose to take her
after having her become healthy for six months or why we
were encouraged to decorate the nursery.

None of our closest friends and family believed she would die. I finally had to pull all of them together. I had an "end-of-life meeting" alone with the doctors. No one else came. They couldn't handle it; it was not something that they could wrap their heads around. They just couldn't believe it. It was unraveling too fast. It was very hard to have it happen so fast. We had overcome all these long nights and long days, and now this.

We spent the whole day at the hospital. We came home. We got a phone call. "She's not doing well. She's gotten worse since you left." They were going to have to put the breathing tube back in, so we gave them permission to do so. We drove right back downtown. When we got there, the nurse was in tears. She said, "Catherine, she knows. She's smart. She knows. She's fighting so hard. She's swatting at her tubes."

I would have loved to have my baby around for as long as I could, but I could not ask her to do this. I was not going to ask her to struggle to live once again. She was dying in utero; she fought and lived. She was supposed to be dying on the operating room table; she fought every day for the last six months and lived. And now she was dying again. She couldn't do it anymore. She could no longer fight; she was done living.

She had started out sick and weak, and then she was up to this eight-pound weight with healthy skin and beautiful rosy cheeks, smiling, taking a bottle. She was doing all the things a normal little healthy baby would do. So this all happened so fast and so dramatically. At that point in time, I said, "God, her healing will take a miracle because we are not going to allow any more medical intervention." We didn't feel it was necessary. We didn't feel it was right. We felt that the medical interventions they were proposing were highly controversial.

We spent the weekend with Alexa, and I had my meeting. Then I told my family, "If she doesn't improve by the grace of God in the next day or so, we are not going to do any more medical intervention. We are not going to aggressively do things for her. If her body shuts down or her heart gives out, we are not going to pursue other invasive procedures."

After I explained all this to them, I asked if they wanted to come and say good-bye to her. I gave them all that opportunity. It was Monday morning, February 23. I didn't know then that she would die the next day. When you make decisions like this, you can't know how or when things will happen. Today, tomorrow, next month. You know, the body is a miracle. She had improved over the weekend. She had improved dramatically.

I sat down and sang to her through the entire weekend. The minute I left—it made me feel good on one hand, and it also made me feel really sad on the other. But what could I do? Could I be there more? Could I be there and sing all night? Could I just never go to sleep? No, I couldn't do that, so I left. I told her, "I love you, and if you go home to heaven, I will see you soon. I love you. There is nothing else Mommy can do. I love you."

You know you have to let your children go every day, whether they are going to a field trip or driving, or whether they go to college or to preschool. You know you have to let them go. I had to let her go. Ultimately, they are *all* in God's care.

I was there at all hours in the end, talking to her, encouraging her. While I was home, I would check in overnight. The next day, the nurse—who we loved, who was the one who took Alexa out of my body in the NICU— was to have gone off duty at eight in the morning, but she waited until I came in. The minute I saw her, I knew—it was the look on her face and the fact that she would wait around until I arrived. I got there a little after eight. I hugged her and she sobbed.

The doctor told us, "Unfortunately, unless you allow us to intervene, she will continue to decline." And we chose not to do the intervention. We were not going to have her live another six months on machines when they asserted there was no possibility that she would ever come off of them.

I said to the staff, "This is in God's hands. We have done everything humanly possible. We have done everything medically possible. We have prayed, and He has answered our prayers. He has done miracle after miracle. We have asked Him so many times to let her come home. He is answering our prayer, but it is not going to be *our* home. She *is* going home. We will do whatever we can to make this a beautiful, positive experience. I do not want her to feel fear."

When the time came, everyone was weeping. The nurses asked our loved ones to step outside. Brian and I didn't want Alexa to leave us in the midst of sobs. We wanted there to be singing. She loved when I sang to her each day. I felt strong in God's strength, not my own, and I felt that He was lifting me away from the first two stages of grief: regret and guilt.

We had done everything we could as a couple, as a dad, and as a mom. Individually and together, we bathed her. We were so glad we had experienced everything we could with her. We took pictures. We did video. She was a star. We have lots of videotape of her. As awful as it was going to be—I didn't want little Alexa to sense my grief in our last hours together.

That was the hardest decision of our lives, but we trust it was the right one. Alexa's body started shutting down. The doctor and the nurse were with us, and they were explaining to us what was happening. I wished I would have been a little bit prepared for that. I didn't know what a body does when it shuts down. I had never seen anyone die. I just held her close until she died. We prayed.

My husband and I bathed her, dressed her, and took a picture of us together. We had come full circle, because when Alexa was born, they gave me a little Polaroid picture, and I couldn't even tell what she looked like. I said, "Well, *that* won't do!" For Christmas our family donated a digital camera to NICU, so if a baby is going to die, the family would have a decent picture. Another mom of a NICU baby sadly told me, "I have a little Polaroid of my baby, Sonia, but I can't even tell what she looks like!" Parents should not have to be without a picture of their baby who died in the first hours of life. They may not want it then, but they will want it as they grieve. They will want it down the road. They will want to look at it on the child's birthday and say, "We love you. Look at your little face! We miss you." They are probably not photos you are going to share with others, but a picture can be priceless.

I know Alexa is in heaven. I still don't understand why God had us decorate that nursery! I still ask Him about that. We really are not going to give up on our goal to be parents. We trust that God will bless us with a

I HAVE BEEN CRUCIFIED WITH CHRIST; IT IS NO LONGER I WHO LIVE, BUT CHRIST LIVES IN ME; AND THE LIFE WHICH I NOW LIVE IN THE FLESH I LIVE BY FAITH IN THE SON OF GOD, WHO LOVED ME AND GAVE HIMSELF FOR ME.

—GALATIANS 2:20 (NKJV)

child whether it is ours, adopted, or whatever. It doesn't even have to be a new baby—it could be an older child.

Reflecting on Faith and Embracing Eternity

I share bits of my story one-on-one. I share it with people I meet in stores, on elevators. I have wished I had been as bold about my relationship with Jesus, but I didn't have the credibility. People would look at me and say, "Your life is perfect, so no wonder you trust God!"

Now I can use my daughter's story to say, "I lost a daughter. Let me tell you how I dealt with it and how I've gotten through it." It has given me a platform one-on-one to say, "Look, I don't have all the answers, but I'm here to tell you, I'm functioning in society. I have not been swallowed up by grief, and I will not be. I will be okay, though there are days, there are moments, that are harder than others." I can honestly speak of death alongside of hope and joy.

> BEFORE I FORMED YOU IN THE WOMB I KNEW YOU, BEFORE YOU WERE BORN I SET YOU APART; I APPOINTED YOU AS A PROPHET TO THE NATIONS.
>
> —JEREMIAH 1:5

There is something quite remarkable about meeting a total stranger who asks me if I have a daughter or asks me if I have children. It could be a nail technician or a grocery clerk. Do I say no? Do I say yes, I had a baby at one time? Do I say I had two miscarriages and one live birth? It gets very complicated. But it all becomes part of the therapy and the healing process. I was deeply touched by a very dear friend who lost her baby a few weeks prior to what would have been Alexa's expected delivery date. She told me all the things she regretted—not holding the baby, not bathing the baby, not naming the baby, all of those things. I had meaningful insights, thanks to her willingness to be transparent and her generous spirit.

The morning of the funeral, the baby had an open casket for a period of time, and she looked so beautiful. Very few people had had an opportunity to meet Alexa, so I wanted to give those people who had bathed her in prayer during our difficult pregnancy, during the difficult six months, an opportunity to see her, touch her if they wanted, look at her face and see who they had prayed for—to have their own closure. I am aware most people are very uncomfortable with the concept—let alone the reality—of a baby's funeral. I didn't want those who were not comfortable to feel like they *had* to see Alexa, so I gave people an opportunity to come an hour before, and then we closed the little white casket for the ceremony. I wanted the focus to be on God and the life-changing message of Jesus Christ.

Her mission? I think she touched numerous of lives of those who had never heard about or fully considered the love and peace of Jesus. I think she changed me and Brian. She changed my whole family. She impacted so many lives—she was a living miracle. And she's not necessarily a miracle in the world's eyes since she will not be sitting here with us a year from now or five years from now. In the memorial service our pastor said, "As beautiful as the nursery was that Catherine and Brian got ready the week before she died, if Alexa had a choice to come back and leave the presence of Almighty God in heaven, she would *never* want to. She would say, 'Mommy, wait until you see what God has prepared for you and Daddy. Don't cry, Mommy! I'm so happy now.'"

I believe that with all my heart. On a very personal level, Alexa also helped me get over my fear of death. Face it: We will all die! We hear this, but we don't really believe it. I've always been told to live my life as if I'm dying, but now I really do. I have nothing to lose. I have lost the most important thing to me on this earth. I always used to struggle with the question of how I would ever survive without my mom. How would I survive if I ever lost my husband? I now know how. That fear is gone, and it was negatively impacting what I was willing to do. What I was willing to risk. I want to continue what my baby daughter birthed in *me*. And I still would like to pursue being a mom. That is it in a nutshell.

After we lost our daughter, they immediately gave us a grief manual. Then they gave us a statistic: 80 percent of all couples divorce within the first year because of the loss of a child. I really resented that at the time. That was just not the right time for that information. Then I had two or three well-meaning Christian friends call. It was bad timing. I wish I could have been just a little bit more clear with them. I think I snapped at them. I said, "I don't really want any questions about my marriage!" I regret having responded that way.

I believe I will see her face again. I believe every Scripture I quoted and prayed when I was fighting for her to live. After her death, it all just took on a totally different meaning. I can't believe God's promises part of the time; I have to believe

MY SHEEP LISTEN TO MY VOICE; I KNOW THEM, AND THEY FOLLOW ME. I GIVE THEM ETERNAL LIFE, AND THEY SHALL NEVER PERISH; NO ONE CAN SNATCH THEM OUT OF MY HAND.

—JOHN 10:27–28

them *all* the time. You can't believe one verse and not the other. That's the other thing: You can't believe God only does things here on this earth; you've got to believe His promise that the dead in Christ will rise! That's *wonderful* news!

I really feel that I want to get back into the Word, but it has been slow and very painful because my Bible is filled with tears and memories of Alexa. "Praise the Lord"; "Please let her get through the next minute"; "Let Alexa get through the next day." My whole Bible is marked and is a remembrance of her. I struggle with opening it some days.

Still, my peace comes, I believe, because when I was twelve years old, I accepted Jesus Christ into my heart. Without making that decision, none of the others would have ever followed. So it goes back to that day when I asked Jesus to become my personal Savior. I didn't know what "personal Savior" meant, but now I do. He is my life raft. I cannot even imagine …

Brian and I try not to relive our loss every day. That is where the differences occur. I can talk about my daughter every day and not get sad. If he hears too much of it, he goes into a ditch. He would rather celebrate. He is very good about celebrating her life, and we did on her birthday. We visited her gravesite and had dinner and talked. We did all the things we needed to do. We often look at each other when we talk about Alexa and say, "Without Jesus ..."

Our peace is not from a generic, faceless God, because so many people think about God without regarding His only Son. It's necessary to have a personal relationship with Jesus Christ, with the Holy Spirit to help you, guide you, support you, and encourage you. I don't know how you even *begin* to get by otherwise. We are strong Christians. We are mature people. We love each other and God dearly, and it has still been a struggle. I just can't even imagine how anyone faces life without the promise and full assurance of heaven.

Alexa did so much to encourage the faith of so many. How I love her! Someday I'll hold her again, and it will be so sweet.

*Think of all the beauty still
left around you and be happy.*

—Anne Frank

CHAPTER EIGHT

You:
Adhering to the Battle Plan

*E*ach woman in this book is truly a hero—or as some like to say, a "she-ro." None of these brave women will ever receive a medal, but make no mistake—they are mighty warriors. In lieu of a Purple Heart, they have each been granted a unique facet of God's heart. They have entered into an eternal covenant with Jesus Christ, the Messiah and Almighty King. They have received their marching orders and taken blows along the way, but they refuse to turn back, to give up, to give in, or to give out.

They have fought for freedom from bondage, self-contempt, hopelessness, and painful memories. They have fought for freedom from the mocking whispers, shouts, and jeers of the Enemy. They have fought well and have claimed their right to be called Daughters of Heaven. They belong to a unique sisterhood, a Fellowship of the Broken. Their battle scars have faded but have not disappeared. As long as we live on *this* planet, the battles will continue—emotional, spiritual, physical, psychological, relational, territorial, governmental— they *will* continue.

But for now, each woman in this book has taken her

THE LORD IS MY LIGHT AND MY SALVATION—WHOM

SHALL I FEAR? THE LORD IS THE STRONGHOLD OF MY

LIFE—OF WHOM SHALL I BE AFRAID? ... WHEN MY

ENEMIES AND MY FOES ATTACK ME, THEY WILL

STUMBLE AND FALL. THOUGH AN ARMY BESIEGE ME, MY

HEART WILL NOT FEAR; THOUGH WAR BREAK OUT

AGAINST ME, EVEN THEN WILL I BE CONFIDENT.

—PSALM 27:1–3

position in the battle. Their varied encounters with warfare have both similarities and differences. They have known the darkest side of midnight. They have survived the fires and floods of life's cruel trials. They have seen the face of evil. They have known fear and despair. They have been marked by "hell and high water."

Though each woman has been scarred—she has also been left with a striking beauty mark. Her beauty mark is not cosmetic. It is not always immediately visible, but it is practically palpable. It is the undeniable, irresistible mark of Christ upon her life, and it is beauty far deeper and longer lasting than the world can ever give. It is exquisite and it is eternal.

BATTLE POSITIONS

Barbara—Giving Unconditional Love

Barbara has been disappointed so many times by her prodigal son. She continues to give him the greatest gift—an unconditional, stubborn love that won't ever walk away. Barbara has the beauty mark of **COURAGE**.

> Be strong and courageous ... for the LORD
> your God will be with you wherever you go.
> JOSHUA 1:9

Joan—Waiting on God

Joan has spent many years in the trenches and still remains there, waiting for a miracle concerning her marriage. There are plenty of unsung heroes in the trenches. She waits. Joan has the beauty mark of **HOPE**.

> The LORD delights in those who fear him,
> who put their hope in his unfailing love.
> PSALM 147:11

Maria—Holding the Lord's Hand

Maria has been literally and figuratively hit from all sides. She doesn't live with self-pity or venom. A wise and noble veteran, she still fights a relentless enemy for her very life. Maria has the beauty mark of **HONOR**.

> The LORD ... declares: "... Those who honor
> me I will honor."
> 1 SAMUEL 2:30

Doris—Forgiving Those Who Are Closest
Doris has faced traitors and tyrants within her own family circle. Her heart was broken many times, but her love for God brought wisdom and helped her to truly forgive them. Doris has the beauty mark of **GRACE**.

> Where sin increased, grace increased
> all the more.
> ROMANS 5:20

Serena—Receiving God's Care in the Confusion
Serena has survived being ambushed and taken hostage. Low self-esteem resulted in her being a victim, but God has transformed her weakness into gentle meekness. Serena has the beauty mark of **HUMILITY**.

> Clothe yourselves with humility toward one
> another, because, "God opposes the proud but
> gives grace to the humble."
> 1 PETER 5:5

Tracy—Knowing Joy Comes in the Morning
Tracy has been hurt by friendly fire. She had no idea the darkest battles would rage right in her own home. With God's help, she will pass the baton of faith to seven wonderful children. Tracy has the beauty mark of **STRENGTH**.

> I can do all things through Christ who
> strengthens me.
> PHILIPPIANS 4:13 (NKJV)

Catherine—Living Through Loss, Embracing Eternity
Catherine has spent five long years in a MASH (Mobile Army Surgical Hospital) unit. The sickness and death of three babies have caused her to think a lot about heaven. She's not afraid. She chooses life. Catherine has the beauty mark of **FAITH**.

> We live by faith, not by sight.
>
> 2 CORINTHIANS 5:7

These seven brave souls are in a line of countless others who have taken their positions in the war called life. That sounds so grim. Is it a war that involves *everyone*? I'm afraid the answer is *yes*. Scripture is clear that we will each face the devastation of the "battle that rages" as long as we have breath. From the beginning of Genesis through today, not much has changed insofar as the depravity of the human condition and the unforeseen tragedies that drop into our lives like bombs in the night. As I write this, our country is at war. Soldiers always refer to war as being "hell." Thankfully, most of us will never experience firsthand the ravages of what *that* kind of war does to the body and soul. However, each of us *will* experience firsthand what the body and soul will suffer as a result of living in a fallen world. What or who would motivate *anyone* to press on?

It's Jesus. The literal "good news" is Jesus. He suffered the ultimate battle scars:

> A bruised head.
> A swollen face.
> A beaten body.
> A lanced side.
> Nail-pierced hands and feet.

The Bible tells us He was led like a lamb led to the slaughter. He died so that we could live. He overcame the world, He overcame the war, and He *will* heal every wound. He is the ultimate liberator! God can and does create beauty from ashes. Jesus lived and died so there would be redemption after the fall, dawn after darkness, and resurrection after death.

Those who believe in Him and who call on His name will surely see their battle scars transformed into beauty marks. They will have quite a hero's welcome in heaven, and they will experience unspeakable joy in that grand homecoming parade. They will celebrate in the New Jerusalem, where there will be no more sorrow or sickness or sin. They *will* see Jesus and celebrate His faithfulness.

He is the bridegroom who keeps His covenants.
He is the father who provides guidance.
He is the friend who is always there.
He is the hope and the healing.
He is the reason for living.
He is the strong tower.
He is the helper.
He is God.

Do you know Him like that?

If He seems far off, then ask Him to come near.
If He is near, then ask Him to come in.
If He is in you, then ask Him to be your friend and guide.
If He is your friend and guide, then ask Him to also be your love.
If He is your love, then ask Him to be the absolute love of your life: your delight, your rest, your peace, your haven, your hope, your joy, your destiny. He loves to be asked, addressed, invited, included, investigated.

Do you know Him? Or do you simply know *about* Him? God calls to each one of us. How will we respond? When I responded to Him many years ago, I had no way of knowing what battle scars awaited me, nor did I anticipate the beauty marks that would emerge as a result. Today, I am deeply inspired and greatly encouraged to display those beauty marks. Maybe like me, you too possess a few deep beauty marks of a Christian, but there are certainly more we would love to have, like the sweet fruits of the Spirit listed in Galatians 5:22–23— love, joy, peace, patience, kindness, goodness, faithfulness, gentleness, and self-control. You can never have too many spiritual beauty marks!

SEARCH ME, O GOD, AND KNOW MY HEART; TEST ME AND KNOW MY ANXIOUS THOUGHTS. SEE IF THERE IS ANY OFFENSIVE WAY IN ME, AND LEAD ME IN THE WAY EVERLASTING.

—PSALM 139:23–24

Of all the feedback I received from my last book, *Leap of Faith,* most comments had to do with one section in particular, in which I expounded on the lessons found in Joshua 3. There we find the Israelites facing a daunting obstacle called the River Jordan. Many men and women have generously e-mailed, written letters, or personally shared about crossing their own "river of impossibility," and that correspondence has given me a lot to think about. What is it that causes some people to persevere through hardships, while others seem to be swallowed by forces and circumstances that cannot be foreseen or controlled? And how about the adverse situations we *can* control or those we actually create? Why do similar scenarios have such strikingly different consequences?

A DAILY "*BE*" REGIMEN

We live in a culture obsessed with looking good and extending our longevity. We are a high-stress, low-carb society. We are also looking to modern-day gurus to help us maneuver through life, and especially through our "spiritual journey." But no popular psychology can ever replace our need for a Savior. Jesus is the *only* one who can truly deliver on His promises and completely satisfy our souls. What the world offers is beauty that fades and "chic spirituality" that will ultimately leave us hungry and yearning for genuine hope and healing.

As I reflected on the seven sweet sisters whom I had the privilege of interviewing, I observed distinctive threads, which are clearly and repeatedly woven through each of their tapestries. There is a "constant" in each of their journeys. What was it that caused these women not only to survive but to eventually thrive? It wasn't a daily regimen of talk shows and self-help books. No, it wasn't "7 Easy Steps" or "3 Golden Keys" or "5 Fabulous Secrets." It was something far more eternal.

Maybe like me, you need to be reminded that God's ways are ancient, current, timeless, radical, and relevant. Maybe like me, you need to be reminded that He is omnipotent, omniscient, and omnipresent. Yes, my friend, there *is* a God, and He has gladly provided instructions pertaining to *everything* that concerns you. Unfortunately, not too many people read the manufacturer's manual, and the results range from messy to disastrous.

I've listened very carefully to the wonderful women I interviewed, and I've learned a great deal. The following "disciplines" will create radical and lasting results for your good. I pray you will be blessed, encouraged, and motivated to pursue a course of action as you learn what those with beauty marks "did right." Here's a summation of what these wise women know for sure.

Be faithful and hopeful in spite of circumstances. **Hold on!**

> Without faith no one can please God. We must believe that God is real and that he rewards everyone who searches for him.
>
> Hebrews 11:6 (cev)

Be committed and disciplined to Bible study and memorization. **Dive in!**

> All Scripture is God-breathed and is useful for teaching, rebuking, correcting and training in righteousness.
>
> 2 Timothy 3:16

Be intentional and expectant in prayer. **Speak up!**

> If you remain in me and my words remain in you, ask whatever you wish, and it will be given you.
>
> John 15:7

Be involved and active in spiritual community.
Reach out!

Encourage one another and
build each other up.
1 THESSALONIANS 5:11

Be accountable and transparent with a close
friend or mentor.
Go deep!

There is a friend who sticks closer
than a brother.
PROVERBS 18:24

Be creative and determined to maintain a
good sense of humor.
Laugh hard!

A cheerful heart is good medicine.
PROVERBS 17:22

Be mindful and joyful about eternity.
Get excited!

My soul will be satisfied as with
the richest of foods; with singing lips
my mouth will praise you.
PSALM 63:5

Hold on to His Hand

Jesus suffered the most brutal battle scars, yet He bears the most lovely beauty marks. Every visual depiction of Him clearly displays His hands. And what beautiful hands they are!

Those broken hands are the very catalyst to make us whole. They are the hands that carry us when we cannot go on. They are the hands that lift us when we are faint and weary. They are the hands that reach for us when we lose our way. They are the hands that cradle us when we need to be loved. They are the hands that brought a miraculous touch to each of the women in this book.

My prayer is that the scars of these women will bring hope and comfort to you in the midst of hardships you or a loved one may be facing today. May their resilient spirits encourage you along your way. And may you come to realize the lasting, true beauty within you and around you.

Yes, life inflicts scars. Jesus is not distant from your pain— He was well acquainted with every level of human suffering. Hold His wounded hand, gaze at the pure love that hung on a cross, and ponder the stone that rolled away. You'll be awed and delighted as your battle scars become beauty marks. Trust God to do that for you. He promises He will. Get ready ...

> No eye has seen, no ear has heard, no mind
> has conceived what God has prepared
> for those who love him.
>
> 1 Corinthians 2:9

The Year of the Lord's Favor

[God will] comfort all who mourn, and provide for those who grieve ... to bestow on them a crown of beauty instead of ashes, the oil of gladness instead of mourning, and a garment of praise instead of a spirit of despair. They will be called oaks of righteousness, a planting of the LORD for the display of his splendor.... Instead of their shame [they] will receive a double portion, and instead of disgrace they will rejoice in their inheritance ... and everlasting joy will be theirs.

—ISAIAH 61:2–3, 7

An Invitation

Dear friend, I hope you have been encouraged by these true stories of those who have had the resolve to rise above their painful circumstances. Maybe your life is moving along pretty smoothly, or maybe you're thinking these stories pale in comparison to the hardships you have faced. Whether your life seems like a sunny beach or a stormy monsoon, it's important to know how to get to high and dry ground. What or who is your lifeline? Where do you turn for help?

Jesus said, "Come to me, all you who are weary and burdened, and I will give you rest. Take my yoke upon you and learn from me, for I am gentle and humble in heart, and you will find rest for your souls. For my yoke is easy and my burden is light" (Matt. 11:28–30).

Jesus was born for us (Merry Christmas), He died for us (Good Friday), and He rose to give us eternal life (Happy Easter). He left His Father's side and the perfect bliss of heaven to bring hope and healing and triumph to every human being. But He is gentle and will not force Himself upon you (the way some people may have). He promises that if we seek Him, we will find Him, and that if we open our hearts to Him, He will gladly enter in. He even offers to eat with us—an irresistible invitation if you love to be at a table overflowing with life and laughter. Yes, communing with Jesus Christ is the ultimate banquet. Jesus invites you to live with Him for all eternity. Won't you explore that possibility? It's the single most important invitation you will *ever* accept or decline. You're invited. Want to come?

For more information, check out www.needhim.com or dial toll free 1-888-needhim.

If you have a little extra time on your hands, I also recommend the following Web sites:
www.growinginchrist.com
www.theinterviewwithgod.com
www.knowinggod.org

Readers' Guide

For Personal Reflection or
Group Discussion

You who sit down in the High God's presence, spend
the night in Shaddai's shadow,
Say this: "GOD, you're my refuge.
I trust in you and I'm safe!"
That's right—he rescues you from hidden traps,
shields you from deadly hazards.
His huge outstretched arms protect you—
under them you're perfectly safe;
his arms fend off all harm.
Fear nothing—not wild wolves in the night,
not flying arrows in the day,
Not disease that prowls through the darkness,
not disaster that erupts at high noon.
Even though others succumb all around,
drop like flies right and left,
no harm will even graze you.
You'll stand untouched, watch it all from a distance,
watch the wicked turn into corpses.
Yes, because GOD's your refuge,
the High God your very own home,
Evil can't get close to you,
harm can't get through the door.
He ordered his angels
to guard you wherever you go.
If you stumble, they'll catch you

—Psalm 91:1–12

Readers' Guide

$\mathcal{A}$s you've read this book, or at least selected chapters, you've had the opportunity to meet some special women. Each of them has chosen to be vulnerable about even the touchiest subjects ... sometimes painful subjects. They have allowed us to listen in on their private reflections. To see their strengths and weaknesses. To feel their pain and joy. And to recognize the amazing things that God has done and is still doing in their lives and in the lives of people around them.

Some of the "stuff" they reveal isn't pretty. Much of it challenged these women to the core, forcing them to discover many things about themselves, other people, and God.

Why did these difficult things happen? Why are they still happening to women everywhere? There are no easy answers. As each woman affirms, however, God is faithful. He loves each of us, is with each of us always, and will never let us down. No, His timing isn't necessarily our timing. His ways are not our ways. But as we face life's challenges, He offers the peace and hope, love and joy that can only come through a personal relationship with Him.

Perhaps you picked up this book because you were curious. Or because you, too, face or have faced difficult challenges. The following discussion questions are simply a tool that you, or a group of people, can use to think through and/or discuss some of the issues raised in these personal stories.

Feel free to spend more time on one question than another. Ask God to make Himself more real to you as, perhaps, you find yourself connecting with some of these women and what they experienced. Jesus, after all, experienced the battle firsthand when He came to earth to liberate humankind from their wrongdoing. He is in the redemption business, creating beauty marks from battle scars. He alone can completely satisfy the soul and help us not only survive but thrive.

Depending on where you are in your personal journey, you may choose to discuss aspects of this book with a close friend, pastor, or even a trained counselor—particularly if unresolved inner issues are surfacing.

God knows you, loves you, and has much to teach all of us through His Word and the stories of people like these women. Accept, with a smile, the treasure of themselves that these women offer you, and take time to explore more of what God has for you and your loved ones. Review the suggestions at the end of chapter eight.

And whatever you do, take time to discover and receive the "beauty marks" only God can give—the undeniable, irresistible mark of Christ that lasts for eternity.

CHAPTER 1:
BARBARA—WAITING ON GOD

1. Why do so many people like Jeff eventually "self-medicate"?

2. What did you think of Jeff's experience with something demonic in the corner of his room? Why? Why is the blood of Calvary so powerful in such situations?

3. Why is denial so common when a parent first learns that his or her child is on drugs?

4. Often the church comes down hard on a parent whose child is in trouble. Why is the church's judgment often more common than love?

5. Barbara keeps waiting for God to "capture Jeff's heart." Why do you think she keeps waiting?

6. Why is it sometimes best to let a child suffer the consequences of his or her bad behavior?

7. Just as God is training Barbara through her difficulties, He uses difficulties to teach us. Share a time in your life when you have claimed a promise of God and received the hope and joy only He can provide.

8. What do you think Barbara meant when she said, "The Word is my life"?

9. Do you believe it is possible to have the abundant life God promises when many aspects of your life are incredibly difficult? Why or why not?

Chapter 2:
Joan—Giving Unconditional Love

1. Why do you think difficulties, such as those Joan faced soon after her marriage, often motivate people to know God?

2. Were you surprised that Leo quit drinking for a year after Joan left him for twenty-four hours? Why or why not?

3. Why can a best friend make a real difference when someone is hurting deeply?

4. What happens when people keep stress inside and pretend everything is okay?

5. Joan stayed in her marriage when another woman might have left. How can a spouse know what to do in that type of situation?

6. Reread Ephesians 6:13. What does it mean "to stand"?

7. Do you think Joan was right to work more on being the spouse Leo needed rather than focusing on his shortcomings?

8. How did Joan's view of God change as the years passed?

CHAPTER 3:
MARIA—HOLDING THE LORD'S HAND

1. Maria mentioned that sometimes she has felt betrayed by God and has had to focus on God's promises. Describe a time when you or a loved one felt betrayed by God.

2. Do you think Maria should have remained with her husband after he began abusing her? Why or why not? When is it reasonable to leave an abusive spouse?

3. Why is Maria so sad now that she realizes she didn't have to suffer from all her husband's abuse?

4. Was Maria right to threaten her husband with the same kinds of things he had threatened her with? Why or why not?

5. What, according to Maria, helped her get through the troubles that kept surfacing in her life? Where did her peace come from?

6. After Albert died, what did Maria learn about God?

7. What role did forgiving Albert play in Maria's healing? Where does bitterness come from, and why is it so damaging?

8. Do you agree or disagree with Maria's position that God will heal her physically? Why or why not? Why do some people in her situation die even though they are trusting God for healing?

9. How does God use our suffering to reach other people with the message of Christ? If you are using this guide in a group and feel comfortable doing so, share an example from your life.

CHAPTER 4:
DORIS—FORGIVING THOSE WHO ARE CLOSEST

1. What did you feel as you read about the abuse Doris suffered as a child?

2. How can we overcome views of God that aren't accurate but are based on bad experiences with our earthly fathers?

3. Both Michelle and Julie married angry, violent men and later divorced them, and other bad cycles continued. How can cycles like this be broken?

4. How did the certain hope of heaven help Doris deal with Julie's death?

5. Why is unforgiveness so damaging, especially in family relationships? What steps did Doris take to deal with that issue in her family?

6. What suggestions did Doris offer a parent who has a rebellious teenager?

7. How does Isaiah 55:9 relate to all the pain Doris and other family members have experienced?

8. Why do we sometimes have to *will* to do the right things God wants us to do?

9. In practical terms, how can we live out the truth that nothing can separate us from the love of God that is in Christ Jesus? To be more than conquerors through His power?

10. Why is it important for each of us, like Doris, to realize that we are God's beloved children?

CHAPTER 5:
SERENA—RECEIVING GOD'S CARE IN THE CONFUSION

1. Reread the quote by Oswald Chambers at the beginning of this chapter. Do you agree or disagree with him? Why?

2. What are some of the ways in which people like Serena hide their low self-esteem?

3. Why do people often overlook signals of abuse before they get married to an abusive spouse?

4. Today, how might someone like Serena face mental illness in her spouse much earlier?

5. What tips did Serena give for dealing with a mentally ill spouse?

6. How can a person learn to distinguish good advice from bad, and know God's will concerning a particular situation?

7. Why is it important for us to gain our self-worth from God, rather than from what other people think of us?

8. If we each prayed the following prayer, how might our lives be different? "Lord, I offer my life to You, everything I've been through. Use it for Your glory."

CHAPTER 6:
TRACY—KNOWING JOY COMES IN THE MORNING

1. What "signals" did Tracy overlook as she dated Rick?

2. How can a person know whether or not "God's voice" is revealing truth to him or her?

3. Why is addiction to pornography so damaging?

4 At least in its early stages, why is anorexia difficult to diagnose?

5. As Tracy's family situation worsened, how did God demonstrate His faithfulness through the body of Christ?

6. How would you have responded if, like Tracy, you discovered your husband was having another affair—with a good friend of yours?

7. In hindsight, what might Tracy and the pastor have done when Rick confessed how suicidal he was?

8. Why do you think Tracy found mentors to help her parent her children?

9. As Tracy worked through her anger, what did she discover about the need to keep forgiving Rick?

10. When we realize that God is faithful and good, what effect might that have on our responses to difficult things?

CHAPTER 7:
CATHERINE—LIVING THROUGH LOSS, EMBRACING ETERNITY

1. What kinds of comments can be more hurtful than helpful after a miscarriage?

2. What effects did the miscarriage have on Catherine's faith in God?

3. In what ways did Catherine and Brian's experience open up opportunities for her to connect with other women who had faced similar situations?

4. Catherine defined faith as "a quiet, confident assurance that God is going to do what is right for you, even though you may not understand it, ... appreciate it, ... want it." What do you think of this definition? Why?

5. Although Catherine didn't talk much about it, Brian and her mother also experienced deep pain after the first miscarriage. What kind of pain do you think they felt? Why?

6. What did Catherine learn about taking one day at a time?

7. How valuable is prayer, whether or not a person is facing a crisis?

8. In what ways has God used Brian and Catherine to touch the lives of other people in special ways?

10. What did you feel and think about as you read the final pages of this chapter?

11. How has Alexa's death influenced Catherine's view of death?

CHAPTER 8:
YOU—ADHERING TO THE BATTLE PLAN

1. Why is it important for each of us to get into the "battle" and claim our right to called Daughters of Heaven?

2. What are some of the beauty marks the women who shared in this book have received? Where do these marks come from?

3. Which of these women's stories connected with you in a special way? Why?

4. How have these women's stories influenced your view of yourself, other people, and/or God?

5. What's the difference between knowing God and knowing *about* Him?

6. What hope does God offer us through His Word? Through His Spirit living within every Christian?

7. Why did Jesus become a human being and end up dying on a cross?

8. Do you know the Jesus described in this chapter … and in the stories of these women? If not, what is holding you back from starting a special relationship with Him today?

Additional copies of *FROM BATTLE SCARS TO BEAUTY MARKS* are available wherever good books are sold.

If you have enjoyed this book,
or if it has had an impact on your life,
we would like to hear from you.

Please contact us at:

LIFE JOURNEY
Cook Communications Ministries, Dept. 201
4050 Lee Vance View
Colorado Springs, CO 80918

Or at our Web site: www.cookministries.com

LIFE JOURNEY®
Bringing Home the Message for Life